Sola Gratia
By Grace Alone

KARL DEBOESER

ILLUSTRATIONS BY CATHERINE DEBOESER

Fulton Books, Inc.
Meadville, PA

Published by Fulton Books 2021

ISBN 978-1-63710-762-1 (paperback)
ISBN 978-1-63710-763-8 (digital)

Printed in the United States of America

PROLOGUE

In many ways, it *was* the worst of times. Medieval times.

Some say *today* is the worst of times. Definitely *not* the best of times!

Inevitably, every person perceives life from a subjective and ego-centric vantage point. There is a natural tendency to think our troubles are the absolute worst. But certainly, the insight expressed in the Bible, in the Book of Ecclesiastes, is true:

> All things are wearisome,
> more than one can express;
> the eye is not satisfied with seeing,
> or the ear filled with hearing.
> What has been is what will be
> And what has been done is what will be done;
> there is nothing new under the sun.
> Is there a thing of which it is said,
> "See, this is new"?
> It has already been,
> In the ages before us.

> "…it was the age of wisdom, it was the age of foolishness, it was the epoch of belief, it was the epoch of incredulity, it was the season of light, it was the season of darkness, it was the spring of hope, it was the season of despair…"
> (Charles Dickens, 1859, *A Tale of Two Cities*)

Undeniably, there *has* been a time like this, when a measure of light has had the power to assail the night of hopelessness and sorrow...the power to transform, to heal, and to redeem.

This is an interwoven story, with colorful threads both ancient and modern, embroidered together in a patterned, literary quilt—a blanket of interlaced fibers and bolstering cloth.

It is an offering of wisdom and hope in a troubled, chaotic world. A chirpy finch fluttering in a cheerless, dismal prison cell.

CHAPTER 1

Maritza "The Lamp"

Life is a conundrum. Every day, ordinary people contend with perplexing and troubling issues and situations which others have similarly faced throughout the ages. It has been a ubiquitous struggle, spanning generations—to survive (first and foremost), to fix, to learn, to experience, to grow, and to be fulfilled...before time runs out. Might one even be remembered?

In a mid-sized, northeastern urban community in the United States, a Lutheran pastor, Maritza Lampara, ministers to her church family. She enjoys her work. Over time, she has been drawn to her vocation within the context of important philosophical and theological questions: Why were we created and by whom? What or who is God? How can I inspire others to do the right thing? What is the "right" thing? Can we earn God's favor by doing good for others? What is the purpose of suffering? How can I hearten those living with disappointment, fear, and tragedy? How can I make the most out of this gift of life?

She has only the best of intentions.

For many years, she has been particularly intrigued by and interested in the reform-minded former monk, Martin Luther (not surprising since she is Lutheran after all), who risked everything, even his own life, to stand up against corruption and religious wrongheadedness. She has extensively studied his writings and others' commentaries about him in college and in seminary, and at other times, in preparation for classroom discussions and sermons. He was conflicted and iron willed, and sometimes wrongheaded himself—an imperfect and tenacious man of his time who utilized his intellectual talents, debating ability, and his deep love for the church to ignite reform of an archaic religious system exploited by the privileged and powerful.

Not surprisingly, even a religious leader like Luther was not immune to troublesome ambiguities and ironies. In fact, anyone who is seeking to make sense of it all by studying history and Luther is going to encounter roadblocks, detours, and contradictions. It's just the nature of things. Life is complicated. Human beings are flawed; they disappoint. Even the most exemplary among us are *simul iustus et peccator*…at the same time, both virtuous and imperfect, both righteous and sinful. Martin Luther fit this description.

In some ways, like Luther, Maritza is driven toward improvement, toward perfection—in herself, her marriage, her church…and especially, in her son. She cannot resist an occasion to try to fix what is broken. Sometimes, she marvels at others' disinclination to want to make their lives better; they simply accept things as they are. Why would anyone be concerned about other people anyway? It's simply her nature. She can't help being helpful. Her helpfulness has conditioned some of her congregants to think that she has the capacity and wherewithal to fix their problems. Of course, this is quite impossible; it can be a disappointment for the sheep of her flock when they realize this.

There are times when she gets knocked down, when she feels deflated and discouraged, when darkness overwhelms the light. It is during these times that she draws inspiration from the Bible, especially from chapter 61 of the book of Isaiah:

> The spirit of the Lord God is upon me,
> Because the Lord has anointed me;
> He has sent me to bring good news to the oppressed,
> To bind up the brokenhearted
> To proclaim liberty to the captives,
> And release to the prisoners;
> To proclaim the year of the Lord's favor,
> And the day of vengeance of our God;

To comfort all who mourn;
To provide for those who mourn in Zion—
To give them a garland instead of ashes,
The oil of gladness instead of mourning,
The mantle of praise instead of a faint spirit.

CHAPTER 2

Life Is a Game

He is a preacher's kid. A gifted, highly intelligent young man, Kyle Tannenberg is, to a certain extent, typical of his time and place—an eighteen-year-old teetering on the cusp between childish self-centeredness and early adulthood. He has been raised and taught in a good Christian home, surrounded by encouragement, joy, positivism, and genuine love. Secular society has pulled and poked at him, causing him to question the validity of all that "church stuff," as he refers to it. Wanting to be part of the popular crowd at public school has made him reluctant to share what he's been taught about religion and about God. His secular exposure and programming have contradicted his upbringing—a stark contrast compared to the church's traditional values and moral guideposts. One could posit that the devil himself has been trying to seduce this impressionable, vulnerable young soul to the sinister side of being. His humanity is defined partly by his desire to be liked, admired, and included, and also by his susceptibility to the trappings of the modern world—violent video games, consumerism, pornography, prurient TV shows and movies, and risky experimentation with drugs and alcohol. How does one maneuver past the jeering, sneering, destructive powers of evil and emerge a sensible, productive, and principled human being? It is a dangerous road and one which unquestionably should not be traveled alone. The secret is to travel life's path alongside others who will not be a harmful influence, to choose to be with others who are positive role models and who share a common sense of what is right, what is good. Profoundly and philosophically speaking, "we are who we hang with!"

Kyle has known Andrew Goodman from youth activities dating back a few years ago at St. Paul's Church, where Kyle's mother is the pastor and Andrew's parents are contributing and involved members. Andrew is a couple years older than Kyle, and he has struggled to find meaningful direction in his life. He simply can't find anything which interests him—not a career or even a girlfriend. Consequently, he is anxiously treading water in a polluted sea filled with turbulent waves of seductive, fantastical distractions. Some have observed that, in today's virtually preoccupied world, boys seem to mature more slowly than girls. Manhood is often reached not at age eighteen or twenty-one, but rather at twenty-eight or even age thirty. Fantasy, for many, is an irresistible diversion away from intentional, meaning-ful, connected relationships—a convenient escape from confronting the difficulties and anxieties in life. The movie industry, video game makers, porn peddlers, and drug companies have preyed upon this adolescent vulnerability and reaped billions of dollars in the process. Illegal drug dealers have also fed this human frailty, causing excru-ciating agony, grief, and devastation in families to the detriment of civilized society.

Andrew has always been somewhat malleable. Some months ago, he surrendered to the temptation of pain-dulling drugs, not realizing their crushingly addictive power might destroy him and his family. He is living in a seemingly inescapable rut, and to affirm his pitiable circumstance, he tends to drag others down along with him. Surrounding himself with other "losers" is an easy road which in a twisted way, allows him to feel better about himself. Kyle has an ill-fated lapse in judgment and associates with Andrew. An air of a little danger and a sense of being slightly rebellious lure Kyle into Andrew's venus flytrap.

After school one afternoon, Kyle meets Andrew at his apartment to resume playing "Resistance: Fall of Man" on his PlayStation 3.

Kyle asks, "Hey man, how's it going? Ready to kick some Chimera butt?"

"Absolutely!" Andrew responds. "We're gonna set some new records today."

They feverishly set about playing the violent game while holding the plastic controllers firmly and yet effortlessly. The colored buttons and joysticks are like bionic extensions of their hands and minds, allowing them to maneuver skillfully through the maze of treacherous obstacles and armed saboteurs.

Andrew asks, "Hey, wanna try something different?"

"What do you mean?" Kyle asks.

"Smoking pot makes gaming that much more interesting and amazing. It takes you to a whole new dimension; you feel like you're totally inside the game, and it makes you kind of a super warrior. Here, just give it a try. It can't hurt you."

"Smells awful," Kyle says. "Like a friggin' skunk!"

"You get used to it," Andrew responds. "Here, you take a deep drag and then hold it for five to ten seconds. Like this."

Kyle is apprehensive as he watches Andrew, who then hands him the joint. "Like this?" he asks. He does as Andrew has instructed, except he isn't able to hold his breath before coughing uncontrollably. "Oh, yeah. This is *great* fun!" he says sarcastically. "I don't know."

"Don't think about it so much," Andrew responds. "Let's just keep playing, and you'll see what I'm talking about. You won't believe it!"

They continue to play the game and toke. Kyle experiences the intoxicating and hallucinogenic effects of the THC. He observes, "Wow, this *is* pretty amazing! I've always loved PlayStation, but this takes it to a whole new level."

"Right?" Andrew affirms.

After fifteen minutes, Kyle's stomach growls. He asks, "Why am I so daggone hungry all of a sudden?"

Andrew says, "Let's order pizza! I'm starving too. I have a coupon here somewhere."

In thirty minutes, two large pies are delivered—one with pepperoni and the other a "meat lover's bliss."

The gaming continues. Kyle is so engrossed in the evading, shooting, and killing that he completely loses track of time. He also doesn't notice his mother has been texting him, wondering if and when he's coming home for dinner.

Suddenly, Kyle checks his phone and notices the time...it's nine twenty-eight. "Holy shit! I've gotta get home." He grabs his backpack and dashes toward the door of the apartment. "See ya later, man. We'll meet up again soon."

Once home, he is greeted by his parents' stern words and threats of limited privileges.

"Yeah, yeah, yeah. I know. I'll try to do better," he distantly responds. "I'm sorry. I was with Andrew, and we totally lost track of time."

He climbs the stairs toward his bedroom, stumbling a little along the way. He throws down his backpack and falls backwards on the bed. He notices his heart thumping in his chest and wonders if he's that much out of shape, or if it's the pot making his heart race. Ultimately, he floats off to sleep, dreaming about being pursued and shot at by angry, insect-like aliens.

CHAPTER 3

A Lamm before the Slaughter

His study is rather dimly lit with a desk light providing an introspective and mysterious ambiance—an image evocative of Rembrandt's painting, *Philosopher in Meditation*. Rabbi Aaron Lamm is finalizing plans and logistics in preparation for the upcoming week.

What a crazy week ahead! How will it all fall into place? And there had better not be a funeral flung into the mix...that would really throw a wrench into things! He talks to himself, and to God.

He muses about how he and his congregation have focused intentionally on ecumenical efforts to help those in need in the broader community. They have successfully engaged the help of people in other religious groups, primarily Christian folks of varying denominations. There's the soup kitchen, prison ministry, domestic violence support, group support ministry for families of drug addicts, Narcotics Anonymous, Alcoholics Anonymous, elder care, and quite a few more. These efforts have obviously paid off, although there has been some pushback among people who would rather focus on the differences in doctrinal beliefs. Some say, "Why should we work with them? It just isn't kosher. They don't believe this; they believe that!"

Rabbi Lamm says, "Hogwash and horsefeathers! Maybe it's time to put away the unproductive ways of the past. People will always have differing beliefs; there's just no getting away from it. There is such a paralyzing labyrinth of rules—from every corner— that well-intentioned people have made up over many years, it's no wonder there is so much disagreement. How about if we focus on the basics of helping the needy?

"There is so much wrong in the world, so much suffering, disappointment, guilt, and shame. So much anger and frustration. Isn't saving lives and helping others more important than following some trivial rules? Ha, I'm wearing a nice polyester blend blazer today... mixed fibers, such a rebel! How exciting that people from disparate factions can put their differences aside, or at least focus on common problems and solutions, and work together for the common good! The good Lord must be smiling. He must be! If there's not a means of reconciliation and goodwill, there will be dissonance and discord—sometimes violent, downright hostile conflict, even war. There must be another way. Would more laws do it? Naw! Would more armed security do it? Maybe a little. How in the world can we all live together in peace? Maybe it's just not possible.

"In the good book of Proverbs, it says, 'When a man's ways please the Lord, he makes even his enemies to be at peace with him.' I'm sure the good Lord knows what he's talking about. I sure hope so anyway. I just know that you can't build *anything* from ashes!"

CHAPTER 4

A World of Hate and Change

The summer evening is warm with a gently sweeping breeze. There is a peaceful quiet sporadically punctuated by bird songs emanating from the trees along the boulevard. Rabbi Lamm treasures these late-night, cobweb-cleansing strolls to his residence, only a few blocks from his office and the synagogue. As he settles into a rhythmic pace, he hears a disturbance off in the distance, and it is getting louder, intensifying.

He comes upon a scene of utter confusion and pandemonium—a group of young men are skirmishing, struggling with each other, fighting for dominance. At first, he hesitates, but then Rabbi Lamm moves into the fray and tries to attend to someone who is lying on the pavement, obviously injured, bleeding, and in pain. Seeing that the injured person needs medical assistance, he pulls out his cell phone and starts to call for help. Immediately, a bearded young man accosts him.

Noticing his yarmulke, the young man knocks the phone out of the rabbi's hand and nastily says, "Nice beanie you got there! Why don't you mind your own business? You got a problem, Yahoodi? Better move along, or I'm gonna turn your lid into a frisbee, understand?"

The rabbi says, "I'm just trying to help this person—he's really hurt, needs medical attention."

The young man responds, "Look, Jesus-killer! I said get away from him. He isn't hurt that bad. Leave him alone, or you'll regret it."

Rabbi Lamm continues to check on the injured man, looking for a pulse since he now appears to be unconscious.

"That's it!" yells the young man, and he pushes the rabbi away from the prone figure. Flailing his arms, he shouts, "Get away! Get out!" The young man turns sideways, reaching for something behind his back.

Rabbi Lamm notices this movement, and, thinking it might be a gun, he hurries off, trying to get away. Rabbi Aaron Lamm, the peacemaker, runs away into the

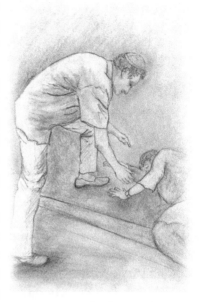

darkness. The young man follows him. The sound of a single gun-shot cuts through the air and reverberates for a couple moments. All activity stops. Everyone is frozen in place, looking stunned. What the hell has happened? The crowd scatters.

CHAPTER 5

Yet Another Violent Crime

In front of the yellow crime tape stretched between maple trees, a female news reporter—Jenny Singleton—with microphone in hand, looking very upset, reports that a shocking crime has just been committed in the neighborhood.

She states, "Details are still unclear; we don't know who the perpetrator is or what the motive was. Police are still investigating. *(Pauses)* I am so sad to report this, but Rabbi Aaron Lamm, a prominent Jewish leader, is dead." She struggles to compose herself. "Rabbi Lamm was well-known in the community…very involved in public affairs and outreach programs. He and his congregation have spearheaded numerous ecumenical efforts to help others in the neighborhood, with a focus on unity, cooperation, and solidarity. This is yet another example of violent and senseless acts which have plagued our city. When will it end? When?" She loses her composure and turns from the camera.

CHAPTER 6

A Time Like This

Pastor Maritza Lampara is in her Lutheran church when she learns of the terrible crime which has been committed in her community, a crime perpetrated against her friend and colleague—Rabbi Aaron Lamm. One of the leaders in the church heard the story on the news and relayed it to her. She is about to go in front of her congregants to preach/teach. In a matter of minutes, she needs to process this devastating information, gather her wits, and focus on her prepared subject matter. Not a great situation, to be sure.

She muses, *There are too many thoughts swimming through my head right now. God, give me strength.* She slowly walks up to the wooden podium and begins her talk with St. Paul's invocation, "Grace and peace to you from God our Father and the Lord, Jesus Christ," hoping that this memorized statement will give her another few seconds to compose her emotions and thoughts. "I'm afraid I have some very bad news. You may have heard that there's been an awful crime committed against a dear friend, Rabbi Aaron Lamm, right here in our neighborhood." People gasp in astonishment. "Can we all pause a moment in silent prayer for him, his family, and his congregation? Let us pray... Amen."

She starts to speak about forgiveness. "So how many times should we forgive someone?" She chokes on these words as the murder of Aaron Lamm crowds out all other thoughts. She thinks, *Forgiveness? Seriously?*

Since this is more of a forum setting than a lecture, individuals start to ask questions.

"About this crime against Rabbi Lamm—do you think whoever did this should be forgiven?"

Shifting in a slightly different direction, someone asks, "Don't you think things are worse now than ever before? Everything seems so out of control and so messed up." This awful occurrence has triggered a larger question for many. Evil seems to be at the doorstep.

"You make some really good points," Pastor Maritza confesses, again trying to buy herself some time to recover. Like a boxer who's been felled with an unexpected left hook, she rises to her feet, determined to respond. She deftly redirects the dialogue by answering with a question, "How do you think people felt during Martin Luther's time? There was harsh brutality, senseless violence, crippling poverty, pervasive illiteracy, widespread fatal disease, corruption in the church and government. There was so much to worry about, and people felt powerless to change things for the better. Generally, the feeling during medieval times was that we, frail humans, are powerless against our circumstances, that our destiny is preordained. *Que será será.* Or in Latin, *Quod erit erit.* People were fearful, irrational, and superstitious. It took a bullheaded, brash, and outspoken monk five hundred years ago to inspire people, to give them a sense of individual power and hope.

"Do you think things are really worse now than ever before, or do we just know more? Because of the 24-7 news cycle, are we more acutely aware of all the darkness in the world?"

An older man interjects, "So we should feel better about how screwed up the world is just because it's probably always been that way? One might conclude that it doesn't really matter what we do; there will always be problems and horrific things going on. Is that a fair statement?"

Maritza thinks to herself, *There's a pessimistic devil's advocate in every crowd.* Addressing the questioner, "Well, that's obviously a pretty cynical view. I'd say it's more like we should understand that our troubles are really nothing new. We're not terribly special in that regard. People have always lived with worry and pain. Can we possibly draw inspiration and perspective from our brothers and sisters who have gone before us? How about from people like Martin Luther? From countless others? I hope you agree that it's worthy of further study. So in preparation for next week…"

Afterwards, Pastor Maritza tries to rationalize in private conversations with several people how God could allow something as horrible as this to happen. And to such a good person as Rabbi Lamm. She privately expresses frustration that she hasn't really given a satisfactory answer to the question. Even she feels on an instinctive level, how or why could God allow something like this to happen? Have we done something wrong? Are we being punished? Was Rabbi Lamm being punished? Why, why, why?

Maritza makes the rounds through the maze of her congregants milling about the church, greeting them, smiling, and embracing many of them. Eventually, she makes her way to her study where she gathers her composure in preparation for the upcoming formal worship service. She thinks about today's sermon topic of forgiveness—a central principle among Christians. She contemplates how it can be such a challenging concept to put into practice...easy to talk about forgiving, but so hard to do. It's also a great topic to preach on; her words flowed effortlessly as she prepared her remarks through the week.

There is no doubt that the horrific news about Rabbi Lamm challenges the legitimacy of this concept of forgiveness...big time! Maritza worries that parts of her sermon might sound like robotic platitudes within the context of this senseless, violent act.

She thinks, *Just when I think I've nailed my message, something else happens to test my resolve. There's always another occurrence which shakes my faith. Sounds like a great topic for a future sermon...but not this one. Gotta keep it simple and straightforward.*

Before heading off to the sanctuary, she glances at her calendar. "Oh, rats! I almost forgot I have a meeting with Mike and Sue Goodman after the service. Such a busy day, this supposed day of rest."

CHAPTER 7

Worried Sick

After the worship service, Pastor Maritza is basking in a mood of relief and humble triumph. There was really good attendance today. She feels as though the service was worshipful and meaningful. The week's preparation culminated in a decisive declaration of faith, wisdom, and joyful noise! Everyone involved—readers, soloists, and the choir—all did their jobs beautifully. She thinks, *What a wonderful blessing this church is!*

Mike and Sue Goodman meet Maritza in her office.

"Is this still a good time?" Mike asks.

"Oh, absolutely," Maritza responds.

As he takes a seat, Mike says, "What an inspirational service today, and an excellent message!"

"Thank you," Maritza says with a nod and a humble smile.

Getting right to the point, Mike says, "Thank you for meeting with us, Pastor Maritza. We wanted to speak with you about our son, Andrew."

Maritza responds, "Of course! That's what I'm here for. I'm so glad you reached out to me. Tell me, how can I help?"

Sue starts to speak, straining a little to find the words. "We are so worried about Andrew. He can't seem to find his way, can't seem to grasp onto anything he finds engaging or meaningful. We've tried to give him direction and support. Six months ago, we helped him find an apartment so he could have his own space. We hoped he would find a job to pay for his living expenses."

"But he hasn't done it," Mike states emphatically. "We're still paying for the apartment, utilities, and food. Hard not to feel like we're being taken advantage of. And even worse than that, we have a sense that he is abusing drugs. I went to his apartment the other day, and it smells like pot. I really hate that smell! And the place was a disaster. The kitchen had dirty dishes strewn all over the countertop and in the sink…clothing, pizza boxes, trash, and clutter were scattered everywhere. Empty beer bottles too. How the hell can he live like this? Our thinking when we agreed to help with the apartment was to get him out of our house, for his own benefit and for ours. His behavior, his lack of motivation was driving me crazy! I was hopeful that if he had his own space, he'd take some pride in it and get his act together. Obviously, that hasn't worked."

Sue continues, "And now that we don't see him every day, we worry…I *really worry*…about his well-being, his safety. We are at a loss as to what to do to help him. Do you have any advice?"

Maritza pauses for a moment, then says, "I'm so very sad to hear this about Andrew. I've known him since he was a little boy, an enthusiastic tornado of energy filled with curiosity and joy. I know his current state is not anything like what you had imagined he would become. It must be so frustrating."

"Frustrating doesn't even begin to describe it," Mike says.

Sue contemplates, "I wonder if we should just cut him off. Then that would force him to make better decisions."

"That really scares me," Mike laments. "I'm afraid that if we stop supporting him financially, he'll sink even further into destructive behaviors and despair. Who knows where he'd end up? I can't even let my mind go there. Maybe he should enroll in a detox program."

Maritza thoughtfully shares her analysis. "It might be premature to get him into a formal recovery program. I'd suggest an approach whereby you have a serious conversation with Andrew. Emphasize your love and concern for him but lay out a timeline of positive steps for him to take. Inform him that he has 'x' amount of time to get a job, etc., and then the financial support ends. He *has* to know his life can't continue like this. It's time for him to get serious about his future. If this approach doesn't work, then it's probably time to look into a rehab program. What do you think?"

Sue and Mike nod in agreement. Then Sue says, "Works for me, but I confess it causes me such anxiety. Sometimes I think I should see my doctor about getting a prescription."

Mike says, "As much as I don't like to take pills, I might even resort to that."

Maritza says, "Hey, sometimes it's helpful. I've needed some of this 'help' myself…only on an as-needed basis, of course." (Catching herself, she thinks, *Hmm, maybe I should have kept that to myself. My mouth runneth over!*) She continues, "Do you think this seems like a sensible approach, a good place to start?"

Sue says, "Sure, I think it makes sense. What do you think, Mike?"

He responds, "We'll give it a try and see what his reaction is. Hopefully, he'll understand where we're coming from." Standing up to leave, Mike then says, "Thanks for listening, Pastor. And this goes without saying, but please keep us and Andrew in your prayers."

"Oh, you can rely on that," Maritza responds. "Good luck. I know this is so hard. May God bless you."

Maritza embraces Sue and Mike, and they leave her office. Understanding that these situations are insidious and tormenting, that families can become afflicted with heartache, frustration, anger and sorrow, Maritza silently and earnestly prays for the Goodmans. "May God be with them."

CHAPTER 8

A Gospel Song

A little while later, Pastor Maritza Lampara and her husband David Tannenberg, a university history professor and part-time church organ buff, are walking outside near their church, heading toward the parking lot, and they hear a lively, soulful song emanating from a Bible church located just around the corner. They walk over to satisfy their curiosity, look in, and listen.

The preacher begins to speak above the musical accompaniment, leading up to the full-volume song. Then the Pentecostal pastor invokes, "God is not mad at you! These things that happen to you are not punishment for the things you have done. It is not Satan or some evil force that is working against you; you are merely being put to the test! How do you respond to these obstacles which are thrown in your path? God loves you unconditionally and supports you in your struggles."

The music gradually builds to a gospel rendition of "Amazing Grace." Of course, the widely recognized message of the song is *grace* and God's unconditional love, even for a "wretch like me." From the vantage point of a different worship style, the message Maritza treasures, the one she lifts up and repeatedly speaks about, is reinforced in a refreshing and timely way. Her faith is reinvigorated by this random encounter. Maritza takes David's hand. They leave and continue on their journey home.

CHAPTER 9

Dinner Time

Maritza and David are at home in their kitchen, preparing dinner and having a glass of wine. First, they discuss the powerful rendition of "Amazing Grace" that they've just heard and touch on the incredible backstory of the song and its author, John Newton.

David observes, "What an extraordinary transformation! For a person to be converted and redeemed, from being a slave himself for a short time to being the captain of slave ships, and ultimately becoming an ordained Anglican cleric who wrote hymns—the most famous of which is 'Amazing Grace'—it's an inspiring story, almost too outlandish to be believed!" He reflects, "Think of the irony...I'm sure most people singing this song have no idea about the history of it. Here's a guy who was instrumental in transporting human souls to a life of bondage, and his life morphs into one of official religious leadership, whereby he writes arguably the most famous, powerful, and inspiring hymn ever written! Pretty amazing, right?"

"'Amazing Grace,' duh!" Maritza points out.

"Ha ha!" David continues, "Think about this, that even today, counted among those who sing this song are ancestors of Black slaves brought to America. I can't help but wonder if redemption for someone like John Newton would even be possible today, given the politically correct atmosphere."

Maritza stops him, "Don't go there! Do *not* go there."

David counters, "Okay, okay, I won't. Ya know, just sayin'. As a historian, as I've studied history over the years, one thing I've come to appreciate is that we should be a little cautious when we look at the past through our present-day lens. There are many things today about which there is little argument whether they are right or wrong—take slavery, discrimination, racism, or giving women the right to vote as examples. For a majority of people, there is consensus that certain things should be advanced, and others should not be. There is not much argument about the *what* but lots of disagreement about the *how*. For example, discrimination is wrong, but how do we identify it and how do we stop it? People should have access to health care services, but how does it get funded and administered? I could go on and on.

"Throughout history people have had a quite different opinion of what was proper, and we can look back and say this specific thing was obviously wrong...and it *was*. But we have the privileged perspective of hundreds or thousands of years. Our visual prism is much more intricate and evolved compared to the simpler two-dimensional world of a thousand yesterdays. That's not to excuse what many did or advocated wrongly in their time, when we can see that it clearly *was* wrong. I just think it's important to assess historical events in context, to give some consideration to the times during which they occurred. And then we must remember everything that happened, the good *and* the bad, so we can learn from the past. So we can be sensible and even a little bit enlightened."

"I see your point," Maritza reflects. "It's very easy to look back and take pot shots at people of long ago. They were imperfect just as we all are. Perhaps it's useful to see the flaws as well as the victories of people, so we understand that human nature really hasn't changed at its core over the course of time. We've all done or said things we'd like to take back. I know I have."

"Oh really? *Not me!*" David replies.

She punches him on the arm.

Their conversation pivots to the awful crime, touching on theological questions—so why *does* God allow such bad things to happen, especially to good, responsible people?

Maritza reflects, "Rabbi Lamm was a unique individual with a special talent for bringing people of diverse backgrounds together to accomplish good things despite their differences. Seems like the kind of person God would want to stick around for a good long time. Just not fair…doesn't make *any* logical sense."

"I know, I know," David laments.

Maritza sarcastically questions, "Is God asleep at the wheel? Sorry, God. Didn't mean that. I just…don't…*understand*."

Suddenly, there's a sharp rap on the door. David opens the door and greets two policemen, "Good evening, officers. How can I help you?"

"Is this the residence of Kyle Tannenberg?" the first officer asks.

Maritza steps up and chimes in, "Why, yes. Is there a problem?"

"A witness identified Kyle near the scene where the murder occurred last night, so we need to question him."

David says, "Unfortunately, he's not here at the moment. But he'll be home later."

Handing David a card, the officer says, "Have him give us a call. Or better yet, bring him down to the police station tomorrow. Don't worry, it's just a formality. We haven't made an arrest yet, so we're gathering as much information as we can."

David says, "Yes, yes, of course. It's just awful what has happened. We'll cooperate in any way."

"Thank you. Good night." The officers turn and depart.

David shuts the door. Maritza lurches backwards, feeling as if she's being hurled into a vortex toward a breakdown.

"This is quite impossible! There must be some mistake. Is someone trying to frame him? No, no…deny, deny. Just not possible. *(She pauses.)* But what if he *did* have something to do with it? What then? Can't even entertain that thought. No, no, no!"

David embraces her as she loses control of her emotions. She sobs, and David tries in vain to console her.

The evening wears on, and Kyle never arrives home. There's no response to text messages or phone calls. The parents are worried and anxious beyond words.

CHAPTER 10

A Memorial Service

The next day in the late afternoon, nearly five hundred people have come together to mourn the tragic death of Rabbi Aaron Lamm, to comfort and support each other. As is the Jewish custom, the funeral was held promptly after death, followed by interment. This subsequent gathering is a public remembrance to honor Rabbi Lamm and to provide an occasion for communal healing. Pastor Maritza and her husband David are there along with many other government, business, and religious leaders. They put on a good face, knowing this awful occurrence may hold greater complications and personal heartbreak for them. In the worship space of the synagogue, people mill about, many hugging each other, many with a look of painful anguish and intense sadness on their faces. There are so many mourners that extra chairs are set up in the aisles, which might not please the fire marshal. But this is a unique occasion; officials apparently don't take issue. A reverent atmosphere of mourning blankets the assembly.

In the rabbi's sermon or *Derasha*, he speaks about this good man who has died; he lists Rabbi Lamm's many contributions and accomplishments. Curiously, he never attempts to make logical sense of what has happened, to answer the question of God's seemingly unknowable purpose for such an incident as this, the senseless, sudden, and violent death of a loving, caring, and involved soul. By not addressing this question, he is, in effect, making a veiled statement. He gives an impression of acceptance, that there is no coherent explanation for us despairing mortals. It seems like he feels he *can't* explain it, so he won't even try. He ends his talk by imploring everyone to live life as Rabbi Aaron Lamm did, to be a good example for others, to help the poor, the imprisoned, the lost.

The Psalm is sung by a female cantor with a rich, deep, and round alto character.

Hear my cry, O God;
Listen to my prayer.
From the end of the earth, I call to you
When my heart is faint.

Lead me to the rock
That is higher than I;
For you are my refuge,
A strong tower against the enemy.

Let me abide in your tent forever,
Find refuge under the shelter of your wings.
For you, O God, have heard my vows;
You have given me the heritage of those
Who fear your name.

So I will always sing praises to your name,
As I pay my vows day after day. (Psalm 61: 1–8)

Finally, the rabbi concludes the memorial service by quoting the Book of Job. He states, "Naked I came from my mother's womb, and naked shall I return there; the Lord gave and the Lord has taken away; blessed be the name of the Lord." He continues, "Blessed are you, Lord our God, King of the universe, the true judge. Amen."

Maritza and David agree that staying for the reception would be too difficult; they've put on a good face long enough. As they move toward the exit, having acknowledged a number of people with polite hellos, several people shake their hands and say, "Blessed is the true judge." Having never been to a Jewish memorial service before, to them, this is a somewhat awkward and inappropriate statement given what they perceive to be an untimely and unjust end for Rabbi Lamm.

Maritza whispers to David, "This situation is God's judgment for Aaron Lamm? Really wrestling with that one."

As they head out the door, Cantor Rachel approaches.

"Aw, don't leave so soon. Stick around and have some food," Rachel implores. "No one should be alone at a time like this."

Apologetically, David responds, "Unfortunately, we have somewhere we really need to be. Our son has this event he's involved with." Who can ever argue about giving priority to a child's needs? "We really must be going. Really nice service. Really great!"

Rachel responds, "I understand, no problem. Maritza, let's get together for coffee next week. I'll give you a call to arrange."

Maritza smiles and nods, then embraces Rachel. She can't even speak as her emotions well up behind her self-controlled façade. Maritza and David exit the synagogue.

CHAPTER 11

The Confrontation

Maritza and David are back at home having a conversation. Son, Kyle, comes home in a whirlwind, slamming the door behind him. He starts to climb the stairs as Maritza calls after him to come into the living room.

"Come here! Where in the world have you been? We've been worried sick! You keep doing this—not telling us where you are, and then finally coming home like it's no big deal. This is unacceptable!"

She presses forward to confront him about the events of the other day… Surely, he has heard there has been a horrific crime committed right in their own community. Does he know anything about it? He admits he heard a little bit about it—his friends were talking. He agrees that is sounds just terrible.

David tells Kyle that the police came to their home looking for him, to question him regarding what he knows about the incident. Someone identified him as having been at the scene.

Kyle denies vehemently that he knows anything specific about what happened or that he was in the area when it happened. The ensuing argument escalates into further pushback from the son against his parents.

"You don't understand me; you're always questioning what I'm doing; you don't trust me; you don't really love me; you just want to control me; you worry that what I do might reflect badly on you in front of your sanctimonious church people."

The parents question the crowd he's been associating with. Is he involved with drugs as rumors suggest? His grades are falling; he's uncommunicative; he doesn't want to stay involved in his youth group or sports.

Maritza asks, "What the hell is going on? We haven't raised you to be this way!"

Kyle defends his friends by saying, "Didn't Jesus associate with the losers of society? The tax collectors, prostitutes, smelly fishermen, the lowest of the low? Why would you or could you criticize who I hang around with? Kind of hypocritical, don't you think?"

"That's not the point, and you know it!" his mother fires back. "God loves everyone despite their faults, but if you hang out with druggies, thieves, and do-nothings, they will be a terrible influence on you. You are going down a dangerous and ill-fated path. We are so worried about you. We've tried to be good parents, to support you, encourage you, teach you, so for you to rebel against us in this way is very troubling, disappointing, and hurtful. Have we failed in our jobs as parents? This must be our fault, I guess. How can we help you? We love you so much and want to protect you from the evils of the world."

Kyle says, "Stop treating me like a child! I don't need you hovering over me like an annoying, noisy, nosy, spying helicopter. Just leave me alone!" He storms off to his bedroom, yelling at his stunned parents, "I don't want to be around you anymore!"

The parents pause to analyze and make sense of what just happened. They ponder... At some point, it's impossible to insulate our children from the darker side of society, but can't children just be children? They grow up way too fast these days. Way too fast...in some ways anyhow. Only in some ways. Much of what they learn about they are incapable of processing, unable to have a healthy and realistic perspective. It's like being thrown in the middle of a lake without knowing how to swim. Or if able to swim, not knowing which direction to swim toward shore. Then we as parents want to be the rescuers because we feel responsible. And we try at all costs to make things right, partly because the potential pain of loss is far too agonizing to even contemplate.

Maritza muses, "So I was thinking about Martin Luther, what it must have been like when he told his father he wanted to become a monk."

David responds, "That's a real stretch, don't you think? This situation is a whole lot different than that!"

Maritza admits, "Well, yes, it's quite different. But it's similar in that Luther's father was badly disappointed in his contrarian attitude. He wanted Martin to be a lawyer (partly for selfish reasons), and Martin was moving in a direction he believed was nearer to God, toward God's purpose for him. Our son is moving away from God, away from what we believe is God's purpose for him. We parents can find just about any reason to be disappointed in our children if they don't conform to our storyline, to our vision for their lives. For many of us, our children are a considerable and essential component of our self-worth. Sometimes parents vicariously live out their own disappointments through their children in ways that presume the child is an organic extension of themselves. For some, having a child is a second chance to succeed where the parent has tried and failed. We can all cite extreme examples of parents who have purposefully groomed their children from early on to be stars, musicians, or sports heroes. Wolfgang Amadeus Mozart comes to mind. There's Tiger Woods. Michael Jackson. It's not always true, but there is certainly potential for dysfunction. Something to think about. I think we have both tried to give Kyle space so he can find his own way, his own passion."

David replies, "On the one hand, yeah, your analysis seems credible, but on the other hand, that really makes *no* sense to me. So Kyle is on a path toward self-destruction, disappointing us, and Martin Luther is a disappointment to his parents because he wants to become a monk. There's a connection here? I think you've had too much wine."

Maritza concedes, "Yes, it is a stretch. If only Kyle's strong will and contrarian spirit could be channeled to something positive, turning him away from harmful behaviors. If only..."

*****

34

Martin Luther in his formative years showed great intellectual aptitude which set him on a path toward a university education. His parents were excited to think their gifted son would become a lawyer—a most respectable career that could raise the parents' status in the community, assist his father with legal disputes associated with his business, and provide resources for their care and support as they advanced in age. So when Martin approached his father—after having experienced a near-death experience in an electrical storm and upon having made a promise to God if he'd spare his life—to inform him that he is abandoning his legal career in exchange for becoming a monk, his father was understandably stunned and disappointed. He probably had thoughts along the lines of, "Why not become a poet, or an artist, an actor, or a musician? The prospects for financial and career success are about equal!" There was no persuading Martin otherwise. Despite his earnest desire to please and to not disappoint his parents, Luther would become a monk. Certainly, he was painfully divided over this decision, but he made a deal with God; he must keep his promise. God faithfully came through for him, so there was no alternative. If Martin Luther did not keep his end of the bargain, surely God would punish him in return.

*****

Attempting to connect the past and the present, Maritza reflects, "I guess there comes a time when our grown children make their own decisions for better or for worse, and there's not a whole lot we can do about it."

David says, "You know, Maritza, we have to take Kyle to the police station to be interviewed. We can't just let this ride."

"I know, I know." She puts her head in her hands and weeps softly. "What is happening? Dear God in heaven, we have tried to be good parents. We've tried to raise him right, took him to Sunday school. We supported him in everything he ever did. We changed his diapers, nursed him to health when he was sick, taught him how to ride a bike, took him to music lessons. You coached his soccer team. This is our reward? Was it all for nothing? God forgive me for saying this, but it's times like this when I can't help but ask, where is God anyway? What could possibly be the value in having to suffer this way? I just don't get it!"

David says, "This is not about us, you know."

She challenges him with hands on hips, "Do you have to keep telling me things I already know?" Instantly regretting her curtness, she apologizes. "This is not the playground I want to play in. I long for a simpler time, when Kyle was little and had a child's exuberance and overflowing joy. What the hell happened to that?"

David agrees, "I know how you feel. I feel exactly the same way sometimes."

CHAPTER 12

The Face of Addiction

In his room, Kyle feels his heart's pace quicken and panic sets in.

"What the f——k happened after I left Andrew the other night? I'd heard there was a fight, a battle over drug territory, over money, or some shit. I gotta call Andrew." He pulls out his cell phone, the revered and contemptible center of his universe, scrolls to Andrew's number and calls.

Andrew answers, "What's up?" His speech is somewhat slurred, and he sounds annoyed.

"Did something happen a couple days ago after I left?" Kyle asks.

"A couple days ago…oh, yeah," Andrew remembers. "These guys from across town, ya know, the lowriders, were tryin' to home in on our territory. They tried to rob me and my boys, so we fought back. Things got a little messy when this guy, this Jewish guy, tried to intervene. He was in the wrong place at the wrong time."

Kyle is unnerved. "I heard someone was shot. What about that?"

Andrew says, "What is this, an interrogation *(stumbling over the word)*? Look, I'm all coked up, can't think straight. Let's talk tomorrow, okay?"

"I think something terrible must have happened," Kyle explains. "The police talked with my parents. They're looking for me."

"What did you do, boy? Ha ha!" Andrew laughs. "Your parents gonna rat on you? Just keep your mouth shut…you don't know anything, right. Say it! You don't know *anything!*"

"Okay, okay…I don't know *nuthin!*" Kyle promises.

Andrew exclaims, *"Anything!"* He hangs up the phone. After muttering to himself, he curses, *Shit!* Then he picks up his crack pipe and continues to "chase the white dragon."

CHAPTER 13

Interrogation

At the police station, Maritza and David wait for Kyle to emerge from being interviewed by detectives. After about an hour which seemed like two eternities, Kyle enters the lobby, looking rather pale and shaken.

"How did it go?" Maritza implores.

"Waddaya mean how did it go?" Kyle asks, irritated. "It wasn't fun, let's just go with that. I didn't do anything."

David asks, "Well, what about your so-called friend, Andrew? Did they ask you about him?"

"Those guys put tremendous pressure on me," Kyle replies, exasperated. "I had to tell them everything I know. Otherwise, they said they might have to arrest me. By the way, shouldn't I have had a lawyer? What's up with that?"

"So what did you tell them about Andrew?" David asks.

Kyle replies, "I told them he was definitely there, that there was some kind of turf battle between gangs over drug territory. Apparently, a fight broke out, but I don't know anything more than that. I wasn't there, thankfully."

Maritza offers, "Maybe God was looking over you."

"Uhhh, yeah, maybe," Kyle reluctantly agrees.

CHAPTER 14

Devastating News

The next day, Pastor Maritza is in her study in the church office when the phone rings. Mike Goodman is on the phone and is extremely upset, overcome with emotion as he attempts to explain that he and his wife Sue need to see her immediately. He barely gets the words out. Maritza invites them to come to the church right away. She is filled with dread.

For the next twenty minutes, Maritza tries to imagine what could be so upsetting to her parishioners, Mike and Sue. She puts on her emotional armor, readying for a confrontation with one of those life-altering situations for which she has been thoroughly prepared by means of formal education and certification, and by experience. She knows it is absolutely critical for her to be steady, rational, composed, and still empathetic as she walks beside her struggling flock when they are face to face with life's devastating blows. What in the world could have happened?

She welcomes Mike and Sue with open arms and a long embrace as they break down, utterly overwhelmed by whatever has happened. Maritza looks on them with empathy and compassion, hoping she will be able to provide comfort and a morsel of hope. These are the moments when a Christian soldier proves her worth.

She thinks, *God, give me the words to say, to help these poor people.*

Mike starts to speak since Sue is not able. "Pastor, our son, Andrew...has died...of a drug overdose. Our only son, only child. We don't know where to start, what to do. Our lives are crashing down around us. We have been blessed with this wonderful child, and for twenty years, our lives have been centered around this lovingly created life. Now it is over. Is this our fault? Did we fail as parents? How and why would God let something like this happen? Couldn't he intervene to prevent such tragedy? What good has a Christian upbringing been for Andrew anyway? I guess the proverbial seed fell on shallow ground. Pastor, how can we possibly deal with this? My wife is a horrible mess, and I'm not much better."

Maritza listens intently without breaking in. She figures it's best to let Mike spill it all out before she tries to have a dialogue. She has learned that her role is not to jump in too quickly in these circumstances, not to try picking up the pieces, attempting to resolve the situation. The only way to be is to be *present*. To be there for people and to be emotionally bonded in grief and pain. Besides, there really isn't anything that can be spoken which won't sound shallow, clichéd, or canned. Silence and body language can be the most appropriate balm for a grief-stricken soul.

"Our son is gone; where is God?" Sue finally asks. She composes herself to utter these words: "My life is over too. Our lives will never be the same."

Maritza attempts to console her, "I know, I know. I think the only thing we can do at this moment is pray. Will you pray with me?" Mike and Sue move closer to her as Maritza offers prayer, "Gracious and loving God, be with us on this terrible, heart-wrenching day. We cannot know the reason for such an awful trial as the loss of our dear son, Andrew. We ask that you welcome him into your loving arms and forgive him as you would forgive any one of us. Show us your love and help us to heal, one minute…one hour…one day at a time. Amen."

*****

Although the idea that he might ever marry and have a family was absent from his mind for many years, Martin Luther and his wife, Katharina (or Katie as he called her), had six children together. In Luther's time death was a constant reality. One child—Elizabeth—died in infancy, and their beloved daughter, Magdalena, who had a "mild and loving disposition," died after a prolonged illness (possibly the plague?) at the age of thirteen. One can imagine Martin bargaining with God to save his dying daughter.

"Let me go in her place. She deserves to live whereas I do not. What can I do, what can I offer to avoid this agony? She is such a blessing to us; why would God allow this tragedy to befall us? Why?" Even Luther, who ultimately concluded that our relationship with God is not a negotiated transaction, likely resorted to a plea with God—*"what can I do in exchange for my daughter's life?"*

Like any parent, certainly he would do anything to save his beloved daughter, Magdalena. Even in desperate times, negotiating with God to exert our will is just not possible. Understanding this, Luther probably still had thoughts along these lines. Such is human nature.

Ultimately, for the Luther family, the essence of the woeful, medieval antiphon played out—*"media vita in morte sumus"*—in the midst of life, we are in death. Martin Luther had earlier composed a hymn based on this well-known, secular quotation of his time, but he altered the syntax of the phrase, concluding that in the midst of death, we live. Yes, there is life and hope, even in death! Perhaps his own words encouraged and consoled him and his wife in the midst of their beloved daughter's passing.

*****

After about an hour of talking, remembering, crying, and thinking through all that needed to be done to address the terrible situation, Maritza helped Mike and Sue make a list of the necessary tasks, the people who needed to be contacted. They called the local funeral home where many members of the church have had their final arrangements administered. The coroner's office was contacted to inform them regarding where Andrew's body should be taken. Key family members, friends, and coworkers were called together to assist and support.

Mike says, "I almost forgot. What about the newspaper? I guess we need to write an obituary so everyone can know about Andrew and about the funeral."

Sue interrupts, "So everyone can share in our shame, right? So everyone can think, *I didn't realize the Goodmans were such awful parents and their son was such a hopeless addict.*"

Maritza tries to be reassuring. "The only people who would think that are those who don't understand the crushing power of addiction, the way it can destroy the family despite everyone's best efforts. You are not bad parents. You are very *good* parents. And Andrew was not bad either. The addict inside him was like his alterego, his Mr. Hyde. That's not really who Andrew was. The temptation to take drugs became an obsession. Andrew was human, just like the rest of us. And we shouldn't blame him for being vulnerable to drugs. We all know how common this problem is."

"At the heart of it, we understand what you're saying," Mike agrees. "Right, Sue? But it's nearly *impossible* to understand why God would allow these devastating things to happen. So hard to figure out."

Nodding, Sue says, "And hard not to have your faith *totally shaken*." She breaks down, softly weeping.

After sharing an emotional goodbye, Pastor Maritza contemplates, *The only way they make it through this nightmare is with the help and support of their family and friends. And not just today and in the coming week, but consistently in the months ahead. It's going to be a long and arduous walk punctuated by waves of sorrow sweeping in unexpectedly, seemingly out of nowhere. It's a perplexing thing how personal loss weaves a tapestry of grief, pain, sorrow, and insecurity.*

She thinks further, *We cannot comprehend why we are subjected to such hurt, to suffering. We can become anxious about when the next upsurge of awful emotions will emerge, seemingly out of the blue. It's a protracted, harrowing road to healing and restoration. There is no quick fix, that is certain. No easy answers. It's not difficult to understand why some people lose faith when they experience tragedy. Based on our intractable belief system, it's easy to think that if God is good and wise and loving and all-powerful, why, why, why would he allow these heartbreaking things to happen? Hard to figure.*

Suddenly, she stiffens, and a cold chill reverberates down her spine. A terrifying thought enters her mind as she remembers the conversation she had with Mike and Sue recently.

"OH...MY...GOD! I told them it was premature to get Andrew into rehab! What the hell was I thinking? I gave them terrible, absolutely stupid advice. And this is the result. Oh my god…oh my god. I am responsible for Andrew's death. I was only trying to help."

Overwhelmed with remorse and anguish, Maritza kneels down in the corner of her study, intending to pray, but instead, she collapses into a fetal position, weeping uncontrollably.

CHAPTER 15

Quid Pro Quo

The next day, Maritza is in her study at home, in a state of deep thought and meditation, feeling a bit numb after having learned of Andrew Goodman's death and after a night of restless sleep. Suddenly, her "constellation" ringtone startles her since she forgot to turn the cell phone's volume down. She glances at the screen—it's Rachel calling.

"You available for coffee tomorrow morning?" Rachel asks.

"I don't know, Rachel. I'm in the middle of a quandary."

"What do you mean? Are you going to be okay?"

Maritza sighs. "I'll be fine. I can tell you all about it." She pauses. "It would probably be good for me if we got together. You're always a good listener."

Rachel says, "As the saying goes, 'a burden shared is a burden halved.'"

Already, Maritza feels slightly better. "I'm so glad you called. Sure, let's meet. But let's make it early since I have a staff meeting at nine o'clock."

They agree to meet at the Jefferson Diner at 7:00 a.m. Maritza feels it's somewhat trivial to be doing anything enjoyable in the context of the Goodman tragedy. Then she remembers what Rachel said after Rabbi Lamm's memorial service—"No one should be alone at a time like this."

The next morning at the diner, their conversation begins with the usual rapid-fire, back-and-forth, icebreaking formalities, conveniently avoiding the elephant in the room, the troubling quandary Maritza mentioned over the phone. How are you? Fine, you? How are things at the church, the synagogue?

Rachel asks, "And how's Kyle?"

Maritza answers, "Kyle's okay, I guess, although I have to say, I am really worried about him, who he's been hanging around with. I think he is experimenting with drugs."

Rachel is astonished. "Seriously? But he's such a nice young man. Why would he go down that path? He has such a good family, great parents, a blessed life."

"It's a mystery to David and me too," Maritza replies. "We've tried our best to be supportive, loving, and yet he seems to be gravitating toward rebellion; he opposes us at every turn. I can't help but think that it's drugs that are making him more belligerent than usual. He's always been a bit strong willed, but this seems different. It's possible this bullheadedness can be a good thing if channeled in a positive direction, but how in the world do we influence that? Especially when he poo-poos everything we suggest?"

Rachel offers, "Well, every child is different, and at this age, they often start to experiment, to find their own way. They begin to step out, break away from their parents. In these precarious times, kids often stray a little too far off the path of safety and sensible behavior. It's scary, no question. I don't know if this is helpful or not, but a family in my synagogue dealt with a potentially devastating situation with a teenage son. He was addicted to opioids as a result of a car accident (long story), and it almost destroyed the family. Ultimately, they employed a tough love approach which fortunately worked…but understand, it doesn't work for everyone. The son had dropped out of school; he lied all the time. He even stole from every member of his family, including his sister. When the parents finally realized that they were not equipped to help their out-of-control son—after months of anguish, fighting, and frustration…and after the son spent a couple weeks in jail—they made arrangements for him to live at a recovery house where he stayed for over a year. Now he is sober, living at home, and working a full-time job. Things seem to be working out, but it's such an unbelievably tough thing. The family is apparently on firm footing again, but for a while, the parents were fighting with each other because they couldn't agree on how to approach the situation. Drug abuse is so utterly destructive—to the abuser and everyone around him or her."

"Wow, yes, that's quite a story," Maritza replies. "You seem to understand a lot about this topic. I've heard similar stories from a number of different folks, even from some in my own congregation. Unfortunately, the outcome isn't always so positive. I've been to too many funerals for young people, even officiated at a couple. Such a waste!"

"Yes, such a waste!" Rachel agrees. "It seems to be the Black plague of our time, and yet people don't want to talk about it. A couple years ago, 72,000 Americans died from drug overdose; it's a staggering statistic! There's just so much shame, regret, and guilt. And the unenlightened still think that the addict should just suck it up! *Just pull yourself together, dammit!* They don't understand that in most cases, the addict wants to get better; they just can't. It's a confounding soup. It's a disease, really. And generally speaking, it's not the parents' fault when kids fall into the trap of drug experimentation and addiction, even though the parents' first inclination is to believe otherwise. You and I have both witnessed it—families from all points on the socioeconomic scale have battled this evil monster."

Maritza insists, "What I want to know is this—why do these 'kids' or young adults feel it is necessary to try these highly addictive substances anyway? Don't they understand that in many cases just one dance with the devil can doom them for life? What are they seeking with drugs that they're not getting any other way?"

Rachel offers, "I have a theory—it's somewhat controversial—and it applies to many areas of our lives, not just drugs. Our behavior as humans is, more often than not, transactional. We do things on the one hand because we expect a certain result or reward on the other hand. These scenarios set us up for potential jeopardy because life just isn't predictable or that simple. I've come up with a whole list of things we do in order to get something in return. Want to hear it?"

Maritza replies, "Of course! *(To the conspicuously tattooed waitress)* More coffee please?"

Rachel says, "There's a lot more, but here's a taste of it." She pulls up a file on her cell phone and reads.

"Everything is a *quid pro quo!* In other words, a this-for-that."

Maritza interrupts, "Is it something like an eye for an eye?"

"Well, a little bit like that. Here's what I mean:

> We want a good job, so we go to school
> We want to be treated well, so we observe the
> golden rule
> We carefully choose our wardrobe, select our
> spouse
> We establish good credit, so we can buy a house
> We drive a nice car to project our success
> To show we're good people, see how we've been
> blessed!
> We want to look smart, so we wear stylish glasses
> We wear stripes and exercise to trim down our
> asses

We ask our spouse to fix the toilet, so it flushes
   right
And in return, as promised, he'll get lucky
   tonight!

People do the right thing not 'cause it's right or
   it's good
They do it only because they think that they
   should

Maritza chuckles, "That's pretty funny! And sad at the same time."

Rachel analyzes, "So the problem *then* becomes, after we've done everything we think that we should to get what we want—and things don't turn out right—we learn that it's all one big deception. It's just vapor, and shallow to boot. We're all susceptible to this. But in particular, I think kids today are fed gobs of information, some true and some false, so they're confused. And many just don't have a *passion*. They're not sure what to believe. They're told by their parents to do or believe one thing; their teachers and friends tell them they should do or believe another. They are so bombarded that nothing good excites them; they can become jaded; they can't sift through the horse shit to find the pony! And they don't even give a crap about the pony! We are all frustrated, sad, confused, disappointed, and worried. So what do we do to dull the pain, to help us cope? We turn to vices…to drugs! Some legal, non-addictive. Some illegal and devastatingly addictive. What's your poison?"

Maritza confesses, "Mine is wine. Only in moderation, of course!"

Rachel asks, "So do you think this makes sense?"

Maritza admits, "Yes, in a roundabout and obtuse sort of way… yes. I really have to think it over though. It's pretty deep."

Rachel disagrees. "No, not really. Think about it—it boils down to: we're conditioned to expect this if we do that…it doesn't work… we get frustrated and disillusioned…we cry…we try something else…we fail…we cry…we dull the pain of disappointment. Rinse and repeat! Simple as that!"

Maritza replies, "A little cynical, don't you think?"

"Well, maybe," Rachel admits. "Let me know if you come up with something better." Shifting gears, she asks, "So did we talk about that matter that's been troubling you?"

"Uh, yes, in an indirect kind of way. This conversation has been really helpful. Thanks so much."

"Good," Rachel replies. "Oops, look at the time! I gotta go!"

"Yeah, me too," Maritza says. "Let's get together again soon!"

They leave a tip and pay the waitress; then they hug and dash off to their cars to face the workday.

As she's driving out of the parking lot, Maritza ponders, *Isn't the opposite true as well? Since there are undesirable outcomes we don't want, there are things which we intentionally don't do?*

CHAPTER 16

Support Group Soup

There are quite a few drug treatment programs available as it turns out, but since Maritza and David are acquainted with the program Rabbi Aaron Lamm (rest his soul) helped to start—Drug Addiction Recovery Center (DARC)—they elect to send Kyle to a group meeting there as a first step. He resists, of course, but when threatened with the confiscation of his cell phone, no driving privileges, and no internet usage, he relents.

"I don't have a problem! I don't know why I have to do this... it's so stupid. I'll go, but it's not gonna do any good. So stooo-pid! I don't use opioids or meth...it's only pot. It's no worse than alcohol, and probably not as bad for you."

As tempting as it is to get into an arm-wrestling match, the parents keep quiet. While knowing there is some truth to what Kyle is saying about alcohol, his argument is quite thin. Considering the extent of alcohol abuse and the misery it causes, yes, they believe it is a dangerous obsession for many on par with drug abuse. It's just more socially acceptable. However, Kyle's rationalization does not diminish his need for professional help. Maritza and David want to nip this in the bud before it gets any worse. The absolute last thing they want to happen is for Kyle to experience the same devastating fate as Andrew. They will do *anything* to prevent that. Absolutely anything.

Although Maritza wants to drive Kyle to DARC, David persuades her to let him drive himself. "He needs to take ownership of this; he needs to do this on his own," David argues. "He knows we're here for him."

After school, Kyle stops at home before driving to the treatment center on his own. He parks, walks into the building, and signs in. After providing his insurance information, he sheepishly walks into the room where people are gathering. There are chairs for twenty people, ten of which are filled. Others are milling about, greeting and talking with each other; many of them obviously already know each other. Kyle knows no one. He is welcomed by a few friendly folks who introduce themselves with a warm handshake. Kyle thinks maybe this won't be so bad; these people seem pretty normal and nice.

The leader, Bob, welcomes everyone and thanks them for coming. "Some of you are returning for about the one hundredth time and others are new here tonight. I'd like to start with first-name-only introductions so we can get to know each other a little, and let's start with the more seasoned folks before calling on any of the new people. Beverly, why don't you begin?"

"My name is Beverly, and I'm an addict. I've been clean for one year and eleven months. I'm feeling very proud of myself, and hopeful."

"Hi, my name is Marty, and I'm an addict. I've been clean and sober for two months. I'm feeling a little tired."

And so it goes, round and round the room. Kyle's anxiety level grows as the likelihood of him having to speak increases.

"Kyle?" Bob urges.

Kyle clears his throat. "Hi, my name is Kyle, and I don't know why I'm here. Well, actually, I do…because my parents made me come. I'm a senior in high school."

Bob continues, "Thank you, Kyle. And thank you, everyone."

"Let me begin by telling you a little of my story, how I ended up being an addiction counselor. I've traveled down the path of drug addiction, headed straight toward the bowels of hell. At first, I was just experimenting; I told myself it's no big deal. I'll just give it a try and have a little fun. Started with pot and progressed to crack and heroin as I sought new ways to dull my pain. Eventually, my circle of friends, my social outlet, became only other people who were drug users. I take full responsibility for my actions, but they were a terrible influence on me…and I on them. This progression lasted a couple of years, and over time, my family relationships deteriorated; most eventually ended. I lost my marriage. My kids wanted nothing to do with me. My longtime friends abandoned me. I lost my job. Everything I valued most fell away from the arc of my life. My focus, my main thrust every day was to get stoned. When I ran out of money, I started stealing; then I started dealing. I spent time in prison. The cycle continued as I pathetically crawled and writhed in the depths of the addiction sewer, bathed in the polluted sludge of arrogance, self-obsession, self-hatred, and self-pity. A few fellow addicts died around me. One day, I finally woke up and concluded, *What the f——k am I doing? Where is this agonizing path leading?* I'll tell you—straight to tormenting evil, hopelessness, sorrow, and *death!* I hit bottom, the absolute deadbeat limit, and slowly began the journey back to the life God intended me to live. It has been a gradual and crooked path, this journey to recovery and *normal* again. To seeing the good in the world, loving others and respecting myself. In a way, it's been a spiritual awakening. By the grace of God, I am here to tell my story. I am here with you, to give you hope and encouragement. I can walk beside you on *your* journey because I have been down the path. I know the way."

Kyle thinks to himself, *Holy shit! That is a crazy story…can it really be true? Duh, yeah. Look what happened to Andrew. He never got a chance to have that epiphany. His hitting bottom was his death. Yikes!*

An attractive, poised young woman across the room raises her hand to speak. "Yes, Carla?"

Carla responds, "I just want to say, I really appreciate your honesty and openness. It's important to understand that hiding in the shadows is not helpful. Being paralyzed by shame and regret is unproductive. You are a blessing and an example for all of us. Thank you."

Bob replies, "That is an astute observation, especially for a young person like yourself. Thank you for your perceptive feedback. It can be excruciatingly painful to look at ourselves in the mirror with total bluntness and say, 'You screwed up! You are really pathetic! You can do better! You must and you will!' This is the important starting point for recovery. Additionally, it's important to forgive…others and *especially yourself.*"

Randy, Bruce, Carol, Bill all share a little of their stories. Kyle is amazed at the similarities in the tales they tell.

After an hour of discussion, Bob provides an overview of the 12-Step Program and draws attention to step one: "We are powerless over our addiction, and our lives have become unmanageable."

Bob expounds, "Out of your experience and by your compassion for others, another dimension of spiritual awakening is possible.

In other words, as unbelievable as it may sound, your journey has opened up an understanding of the world which you could not have achieved any other way. You may not be in a place where you can grasp this, but think on this concept, and pray on it; see where it leads.

"Let's conclude with a word of prayer.

"God, grant us knowledge that we may write according to your divine precepts. Instill in us a sense of your purpose. Make us servants of your will and grant us a bond of selflessness, that this may truly be your work, not ours—in order that no addict, anywhere, need die from the horrors of addiction.

"Thanks again, everyone! I look forward to seeing you next week. In the meantime, if you need anything, *anything*, let me know immediately. Good night!"

The friends in the newly reinforced hodge-podge of wandering and curious souls bid farewell to each other. Kyle zeros in on Carla, makes a point to say good night.

"How long have you been coming here?" he asks.

"Oh, let me see…about six weeks. It's been quite an eye opener for me, very helpful. I'm starting to get myself back on track. I had a boyfriend who introduced me to crack. What a loving and special thing for him to do, right? I'm done with him, and I have a pretty clear vision of what I want my life to be. Life is challenging enough; I don't want to be handicapped by an illicit drug fixation. Know what I mean? What's your story? Why are you here?"

"I'm doing research for a paper."

"No, you're not, you liar!" she scoffs.

"Ach, ya got me! My parents think hearing others' stories about their life-altering experiences with drugs and the damage it causes will discourage me from wading deeper in the mire of drug use. Hearing some of these stories tonight makes me think maybe they're onto something. Gotta say, many of these stories are pretty scary and heart wrenching. Maybe young people like us should be less impulsive about experimenting with drugs. If everyone knew about the potential consequences of drug experimentation, they might be less reckless."

Carla reflects, "Maybe. But our peers get caught up in the moment, ya know, feel the pressure to go along with the crowd. Who wants to be a party pooper? Takes a lot of courage and conviction to say, 'No thanks, not tonight, not *ever*.'"

Kyle adds, "Guess we can't save the world, right? People will do whatever they want to do, and there's really no stopping them. Hard to explain why people do what they do sometimes."

Carla agrees, "Yeah, true nuff! Well, I gotta go. Maybe I'll see you next week? Hope so! Bye!"

They part ways and head home. Kyle thinks to himself how, all in all, going to the meeting was a pretty good experience. He's got a new take on this addiction thing. And Carla's an added bonus, a new friend...smart and pretty. Seems like she's turning the corner, which is one more potential motivation to make him reconsider his drug use.

CHAPTER 17

Looking for Healing

A week later, Pastor Maritza is waiting in her church office for her next appointment, Susan Goodman, who just yesterday requested a counseling session. The funeral for her son, Andrew, was a few days ago; the tormenting hurt from that whole experience is still at the forefront of her daily life. When Maritza saw her last, Susan was a crumpled ball of grief, barely able to speak or stand, her eyes swollen and bloodshot.

Maritza contemplates, *My goal with Susan is to be beside her, to assure her that God is with us, even in our bleakest times, to give us hope and some level of comfort. I can't explain the obvious questions that accompany such an experience—what is the purpose of suffering? Why does God allow such misery?* These questions have doggedly plagued her throughout her *own* faith journey. She thinks, *How can I counsel someone like Susan when I have my own doubts and questions about these things? Maybe this uncertainty in and of itself can be a valuable message. Nooo, she needs stability, not my doubts.*

Susan arrives ten minutes late. Over the next hour, she pours out her soul to Maritza, sharing her most intimate and secret thoughts and feelings about being a mother and a wife. Her whole identity has been invested in these roles, and both have been thoroughly inter-twined over many years. Now the quilt of her life is left with a gaping hole, with an irreparable defect. And although she acknowledges that her husband, Mike, is struggling too, he doesn't seem to appreciate what she's going through, how unmanageable this situation is for her.

Sometimes, she privately blames him for what has happened. Maybe he should have been a stricter disciplinarian for Andrew, a tougher father, like her own father. Guilt and shame join hands with grief and taunt her, encircle her, like a group of sneering fiends. The multiple emotions threaten to overwhelm her, even to destroy her. Such are the ripple effects of evil, of addiction, and devastating loss. Could this be Satan at his finest?

"Pastor Maritza, how can I ever recover from this?" Susan pleads. "I can't see a way forward. I don't know how to shake these paralyzing thoughts and emotions. Every day I wake up, and this nightmare is staring at me from the bottom of the bed."

Maritza responds, "I'm sure over time this will get a little easier. But it's one of those things that we can never really get over. You'll think of Andrew every day...*every single day*. And you'll wish that you could pick up the phone and call him or meet up with him for a mother-son visit. You'll wish that things could have turned out differently, if only…

"It's too soon to even think about this, really, but maybe eventually, you'll be able to provide some support and comfort to others who have had similar experiences. Like with most traumas, the only people who can be truly effective helping others to heal are those who have traveled a parallel road. Just a thought."

"I'll think about it," Susan replies. "Right now, I really need a plan for my own healing. Should I go for grief counseling? Should Mike and I go together? Or would some kind of group therapy be best? Mike and I seem to be dealing with this differently, and I don't think he fully appreciates how this is affecting me. I know he's hurting too. But, honestly, it's not realistic to expect him to fully understand and fix me, even though he's my partner on this journey."

Ultimately, they decide that one-on-one counseling with a psychologist who specializes in grief therapy is the best place to start. Susan thinks Mike will be reluctant to join her anyway, so she decides to move forward on her own. Maritza gives her a phone number for a Christian psychologist who has an excellent reputation. He even takes insurance.

CHAPTER 18

Evil at the Doorstep

Kyle is at the support group again. His demeanor is calm this time around since he more or less knows what to expect. Bob has a way of hitting the issue of addiction head-on, with a genuine empathy and yet an aura of wisdom and authority. Kyle likes that. No wishy-washiness, no sanctimony, no judgment…well, maybe a little judgment, particularly if someone is bullshitting—a common behavior among addicts. As he says, you can't bullshit a bullshitter! Bob has x-ray vision when it comes to spotting deceptions and fabrications. He knows full well how addicts think and behave. A liar cannot boogie dance around Bob; he'll knock the deceiver's legs right out from under him.

As they go around the circle with the usual introductions, Kyle notices that Carla is not there. *Rats! I was hoping to see her again,* he admits. *Wonder why she's not here.*

Bob zeros in on Marty, knowing that he and Carla are friends of sorts. "Where's Carla tonight? Is she okay?"

Marty responds, "Uhh, I dunno. I think she mighta had a setback."

A little testy, Bob continues, "What do you mean a setback?"

Marty answers reluctantly, "Well, I don't know. She kinda had a rough day yesterday. She was in a bad place, so I helped her."

Bob says sternly, "Hold on, hold on! What do you mean you helped her?"

"She needed to calm her nerves," Marty responds, "so she asked me for some 'beast.' She insisted, so I gave it to her."

Bob asks, "Where is she now?"

Marty says, "I guess she's at her place. That's where she was when I left her."

Bob asks in earnest, "Wait, you haven't checked on her? Since when? Are you a f——ing idiot? We need to check on her *now*!"

Bob pulls out his cell phone and tries to call Carla. After a number of rings and anxious moments, he hears her recorded greeting, "Hey, it's me. You can leave a message, and I *might* call you back."

Bob thinks, *Why can't kids be more businesslike these days? Damn!* Checking his jacket pocket for his emergency dose of Naloxone, Bob declares, "This meeting is over. I gotta take care of this and check on Carla. See you next week. Kevin, can you come with me?"

Bob and Kevin dash out the door while everyone else sits and glares at Marty.

"Way to go, bro," Randy says. "Why do you even come here anyway? You don't seem to take this very seriously. Is it just because it's a condition of your parole? You might have killed Carla, you a——hole!"

Marty lashes back. "Lay off, Randy. Screw you! You got a lot of nerve pointing a finger at me. You've dealt doses laced with fentanyl which probably resulted in several ODs. Ha, one finger pointing at me and three pointing right back atcha."

Over the last fifteen minutes, Kyle's mood has evolved from relative peace to anxiety to concern and now, to simmering anger.

Randy starts to rise from his seat to counter Marty's accusations when out of nowhere, Kyle sprints from his chair and launches himself at Marty, knocking him backwards off his chair. The two tumble and roll in a struggle of muscle and rage. As Marty is bigger and brawnier than Kyle, he quickly gains advantage and slings Kyle into the wall while howling an animal-like yell, like a demon-possessed beast in need of an exorcism.

Kyle goes blank.

CHAPTER 19

A Vision

In an instant, Kyle's familiar awareness of time and physical space takes a reprieve. Sensing an odd dreamlike atmosphere, a mystifying fourth dimension, he feels himself being lifted by his arm to a standing position.

Drowsily and nervously, he asks, "Marty, is that you? Get away from me!"

"No, this is Martin. Martin Luther."

"Lucifer? I knew you were real. I just knew it!" Kyle responds dreamily.

Luther corrects him, "No, *Luther*. Martin *Luther*."

"What the...?" Kyle reacts skeptically.

Luther observes, "Seems to me you have anger issues. Take it from me, you have anger issues."

Kyle pushes back. "How would you know? You don't know me."

Luther counters, "Well, I do, actually. And you remind me a lot of myself. Perhaps we should get to know each other a little better. What do you think?"

Kyle considers Luther's proposal. "Well, I suppose. I don't see anyone else here, and I don't know where the heck I am. Might as well talk with you. Explain what you mean by saying you know me. And why are you dressed like that?"

With an enigmatic glint in his eye, Luther smiles as if he's holding back an amazing secret. Ignoring the fashion commentary, he responds, "Well, let's just say I've observed in you characteristics not uncommon in people your age. You think you are smart, and you are, but you are not wise. It's not your fault; wisdom only comes with experience. It only comes with having stumbled on occasion, with having made blunders over a number of years. If we choose to, we can learn the most when we've made mistakes.

"We all stray from the straight path, and believe me, I've had my share of screw-ups. You could call it 'baptism by fire.' If young people like you were wise, the devil couldn't do anything to you, but since you aren't wise, you need us who are old. *Really, really old!* From a caring parent's perspective, the only hope is that one's children don't make life-altering choices from which there is no turning back. Do you understand what I'm saying?"

"Sure, you've got me so far," Kyle acknowledges.

Luther continues, "You are strong; you have a sense of decency. In your heart you want to do what is right. You want to please your parents, and you have a quite promising future. However, you must resist evil in whatever form it presents itself. I have dueled with the devil day and night, and he is a formidable opponent, let me tell you!

Just when I think I have repelled him, he keeps turning up at my doorstep. Evil can take many forms, and sometimes I think he even takes up residence in *me!*"

Kyle asks, "How is that even possible? I've been taught that you accomplished so many good things and against powerful odds."

"Yes, I did get a lot done," Luther admits. "But I also hurt a lot of people along the way. There was no instruction manual on how to reform the church, and there was no way to do it without being tough and outspoken. Or without awakening a tyrannical opposing force which was utterly determined to preserve the status quo, even to the point of aggressively quashing justified criticism. I got carried away sometimes in how I expressed myself—a little too colorful, let's say. I had no tolerance for opposing opinions, and I enjoyed showing off my eloquent, often crass debating ability to drive home a point. That part of me might not have been evil, but it certainly was devilish. Well, no, if I'm totally honest, sometimes it was in fact evil. You may have heard it said that the will is a beast of burden. If God mounts it, it wishes and goes as God wills; if Satan mounts it, it wishes and goes as Satan wills; nor can it choose its rider...the riders contend for its possession."

"So the will is an ass?" Kyle jokes.

Luther laughs, "Yes, you could say that, ha ha. *(Pauses)* So enough about me. What about *you?*"

Somewhat surprised by the question, Kyle says, "What about *me?* I have no idea what to say. Unlike you, I'm at a loss for words."

Luther applauds Kyle. "Ouch! Tou...ché!" Luther turns. "Well, look over there! It's your friend, Carla! Come, join the conversation. Oh, and look, there's Andrew too! Andrew, you're looking pretty good, considering..."

Completely surprised, Kyle says, "Carla? And Andrew! What in the world? Wow, it's great to see you both, especially you, Andrew! I mean, and especially you too, Carla. But what are you two doing here? This is a dream, right? Or is it a premonition?"

Andrew replies, "You might say we are the figurative ghosts of Christmases past and present. Kind of a ludicrous analogy, I know, I know. But I'm the past, because I have passed—can't change that—and Carla is the present; her story is unfolding even as we speak."

Carla adds, "There's no ghost of Christmas future, but that can come later. Let's see how this conversation goes. Let's see if there even is a future."

Andrew explains, "Let me start by saying, in my own defense, I didn't intentionally kill myself. My behavior increased the chances of this happening, but that was not my goal. I got trapped in the stinkin' cesspool of addiction and tried to get others to join me, including you and Carla. Regret is not an adequate description of how I feel. Can you two ever forgive me? I feel so bad for my parents; they certainly don't deserve the pain I've caused them.

"I also did not murder the rabbi. It was Marty. He was afraid the rabbi was going to identify us with the authorities and have us all prosecuted. Oy vey." (Puts his hands on his head.)

From opposite sides, Carla and Kyle put their arms around Andrew's shoulders.

"And I got drawn into the swamp of self-hate and self-pity," Carla explains. "I thought, let me just dull the pain of all that 'self' stuff for another day or two. I'll kick the can of recovery down the road a little farther. It'll keep."

Kyle analyzes, "Seems like we have an intervention committee here. Is that what this is?"

Andrew tries to convince him that it's no big deal. "What makes you say that? We're just mingling."

Carla chimes in, "Yeah, you, me, Andrew…and Martin Luther. What's so 'interventional' about that?"

Kyle lowers his head and looks askance at the three of them. "What is going on here exactly?"

Carla and Andrew lift their shoulders and hold out their palms, as if to claim they're not part of the scheme.

Luther breaks the silence. "So, Kyle, here's a question for you: Do you think there is an optimistic purpose for your life?"

Kyle answers, "Sure, yes."

"Do you know what that is?"

"Honestly, I'm still trying to figure that out."

Luther tries to be reassuring. "It's good that you're thinking about it. It most likely will be a gradual revealing of God's mysterious purpose for your life, so don't expect a sudden flash of light, an epiphany. On second thought, it could be a bolt of lightning. It was for *me!*"

Kyle responds, "Oh yeah, I remember learning about that. You thought a nearby lightning strike in the woods was a sign from God. You promised him that if he delivered you from the storm you would become a monk. Your father was not pleased."

"No, he wasn't," Luther agrees. "That was a challenging time which really strained my relationship with my parents. But it led to an intensive time of study and discernment. I was compelled to consider, over a number of years, what is our relationship with God? Should we try to please God just as we would try to please our parents, to earn their approval? Ultimately, I concluded that there are divine parallels that can be drawn to the parent-child relationship, but the idea of acting a certain way or doing certain things to please God is a hollow ambition."

"This is starting to make sense to me," Kyle concludes. "As I think about it, maybe part of my rebellion is that I want to have my own purpose, not my parents'. The trouble is trying to find what that purpose is. What is my passion anyway?"

Luther replies, "That answer will eventually be clearer to you. In the meantime, your parents are merely trying to keep you safe and true to yourself while you struggle to figure it all out. I'm sure they just want you to maintain an open mind and heart, to be receptive to God's divine purpose for your life. To be sympathetic to God's creative vibration."

Kyle brightens. "I like that…God's creative vibration. Interesting way of putting it."

Andrew and Carla agree, nodding their heads.

Pleased that he seems to be getting his message across, Luther says, "It really works, doesn't it? Within that 'vibration' is a mixture of God's love and his grace, both of which are there for us with no strings attached. Both are unconditional!"

Kyle adds, "I think I'm starting to get it. Have to say, this is a very freeing concept. Thinking that we don't have to do anything to impress God, to earn his love, is absolutely liberating. As I analyze myself, this has also been part of my problem. I've been thinking there's no way I can measure up to my *parents'* expectation of me. There's no way I can be good enough because on the inside, I know I am vulnerable and weak. I know I am susceptible to failure. Deep down, I appreciate that they love me no matter what, but I keep focusing on this idea that I have to measure up in order to please them."

Aware that he may be stating the obvious, Luther asks, "This sounds very similar to our relationship with God, right?"

Kyle agrees and asks, "How come it's been five hundred years since you pushed this concept and people still aren't getting it?"

Luther explains, "There's been more emphasis on having to abide by rules, focusing on religious discipline, doctrine, rituals, procedures, confession, repentance, etc., and for the noncompliant, the customary penalty is the eternal fires of hell! One could conclude that over many years, God's true message has been distorted by religious bureaucracy and autocracy, by leaders who are obsessed with preserving their power, their self-importance, their control over others, the people's money...limiting everyone else's freedom, except theirs."

(He puts his index finger on his chin, scrunches his lips and looks skyward.) "Perhaps it's time for another reformation? I wonder what that would look like."

Turning his focus back to Kyle, Luther continues, "Moreover, everyday people are repulsed by the fact that the messengers espousing a vengeful, angry, and punishing God are sometimes hypocrites themselves, saying one thing in public, and in their private lives, doing something quite different. Not all, but some. Easy to cite multiple examples. When this duplicity is laid bare, observers paint the entire religious community with a broad brush of skepticism and distrust. Really can't blame them.

"There is a better message, a genuinely healing message. It's the same one I campaigned on five hundred years ago, and it is as relevant today as ever before! *Sola Gratia! By grace alone!*"

Kyle takes a moment and ponders the significance of this. "Wow, by grace alone!"

After a few seconds, Andrew adds, "Oh, and one more bit of advice—take it from me. Use your wits, not your fists!"

Carla adds, "Words, not swords!"

"Got it," Kyle acknowledges. "I know, anger issues."

Feeling a brand-new measure of peace as a result of this insightful revelation, Kyle dreamily floats back into real-world consciousness, aware that medical personnel are attending to him. Randy is still there, and he tells him that Carla is fine. Bob got to her just in time.

"Oh, thank God," Kyle sighs.

CHAPTER 20

Analyzing

Alone in her study, Pastor Maritza prepares for her weekly Adult Roundtable discussion. Thinking about how recent events have shaken her faith, her trust in God, she admits feeling somewhat betrayed.

She prays out loud. "Dear God, why is it that I...that I and others around me...have tried to do what's right—we've tried to be kind, to be generous, to be good citizens and responsible parents—and yet you allow these almost unbearably evil things to happen? Are you punishing us for some reason? Feels a bit cruel. Are you standing back in holy amusement, watching while we mere mortals stumble, fall, bleed, weep, and ultimately die? I know...yes, I really *do* believe...you are present when our loved ones are hurting and in pain. When we long to help them in their tough times. We desperately want to insert ourselves in situations, to solve their problems, but it's just impossible. Could it be that your relationship with us is like that? Does your divine heart ache for us? Because even an all-powerful God cannot swoop in like a superhero to the rescue to miraculously fix what is wrong?" She pauses. "Hmmm. Oh...Amen!"

"I think I might be onto something here! Can't say I like it very much, to be quite honest. But as the saying goes, it is what it is... kind of like the laws of physics. How will my congregation respond to a message like this? Will attendance at church continue its downward slide if I share this revelation? Sure don't need that!" Shifting gears a bit, she thinks, *All we need now is a pandemic, something like the bubonic plague, to really put the kibosh on my church. Or maybe it would do just the opposite. Who knows?*

People are desperately looking for answers, for comfort, for healing balm on an open wound. They are looking for a cue, a cure, a call to action. Not sure they can handle this message right now. I think I'll stick with the subject matter for today's curriculum—Johann Tetzel and indulgences, and Martin Luther's disdain for this practice. It's kind of similar, in some ways, maybe…the idea that one could pay money to gain salvation, to erase our offenses, even those of our dead relatives! This idea of getting something from God in exchange for something else (a *quid pro quo*)—it's quite silly if you really think about it. Such folly!"

*****

Indulgences

The origins of indulgences can be traced five hundred years prior to Martin Luther. Early on, the church used the issuing of indulgences as an inducement for recruiting soldiers for the Crusades, to stop the expansion of Turkish military forces and reclaim territories previously captured by the Turks. Recruits were promised complete absolution of their sins if they fulfilled a specific military enlistment. Recognizing an opportunity for some serious money-raising, the church, some two hundred years later, modified the practice by adding a financial component. If someone was unable to earn absolution by doing good works, especially if one's sins were substantial, then paying significant sums of money was a logical progression. The church developed a scheme which specified what would be required as payment, as restitution for various transgressions. The remarkable effectiveness of the sale of indulgences imparted an expanded sense of divinely anointed authority to the pope and other leaders of the church. This exceptional ability to manipulate god-fearing people, because of their ignorance, gullibility and superstitious natures, was, in effect, a means of leveraging their faith against them. Most of these earnest believers were individuals of modest resources. The common folk were victimized by church representatives who ruthlessly and selfishly abused their power and authority. The people's abject fear of God's harsh judgment and angry retribution was a vulnerability which the church took advantage of with astounding success.

The pope, bishops, and cardinals had self-appointed authority to oversee the so-called Treasury of Merits, which was accessed upon the sale of an indulgence. This imaginary storehouse of heavenly treasures, presumably accrued by the deaths of Christ and the saints (since they overflowed with goodness), could be accessed by church authorities and bestowed upon repentant and generous donors to absolve them of their sins. (Pay for your transgressions, have your sins forgiven—some or all— and the church can build a cathedral or commission a work of art or music. It's a win-win!) What's more, deceased relatives, even without their willful repentance, could be released from purgatory with adequate payment. Incredibly, one could even pay for the absolution of future sins!

One hundred years before Martin Luther, another reformer, Jan Hus (sometimes anglicized as John Huss), expressed his opposition to the practice of selling indulgences. As is often the case, when truth speaks to power, when Hus would not disavow his critical statements, he was exe-

cuted—burned at the stake. He paid the ultimate price for attempting to quash this disgraceful yet effective money-raising ploy.

The executioner said as he was lighting the fire for Hus's execution, "Now, we will cook the goose."

Hus replied, "You are now going to burn a goose, but in a century, you will have a swan which you can neither roast nor boil."

That "swan" about whom Jan Hus prophesized was the religious renegade, Martin Luther.

Imagine the infamous friar of Luther's time, Johann Tetzel, the pope-appointed grand commissioner of indulgences, bellowing in the town square:

"Indulgences for sale! Come, pay your bail. What have you done? It's a sliding scale!"

He was exceptionally effective raising money for the church, toward the construction of St. Peter's Basilica in particular, traveling from village to village, peddling his signed certificates of forgiveness.

"Come, take a share from the treasury of merits! Drink of the cup of remission, the contents of which were accrued by the deaths of Christ and the martyrs. Taste of their goodness and have your sins forgiven...for a modest fee, of course! Depending what you have done."

The 95 Theses

Luther had visited Rome, where he witnessed firsthand the conspicuous purpose for the church's broad fundraising activities—breathtaking architecture, ostentatious wardrobes and artwork, grand statues, etc. He fully appreciated why the church unrelentingly pressed the masses for donations. He learned that lavish expenditures included financial support for clerical concubines and their "illegitimate" children. This disturbed Luther greatly. For the church to use the common folk's money this way—money which was often given when they could barely afford to eat, let alone give— was unethical in his view. Against this backdrop, when he witnessed and grasped the full meaning of the sale of indulgences, he was compelled to post his history-changing 95 Theses on the door (a.k.a. "bulletin board") of the Wittenberg Castle Church. He viewed this action not as an accusation or a protest per se, but rather as a means of raising a topic for academic discus-

sion and debate. He had no idea that this "scrap of paper," as he referred to it, would cause such an earthquake, shaking the Roman Catholic Church and spawning a wide-ranging reformation movement.

Once Luther's 95 Theses became widely disseminated, thanks to the newly invented printing press and an absence of copyright law, the spark of ecclesiastical skepticism had been lit and the fire of reform had begun to spread. Johann Tetzel's indulgences balloon deflated, and he was no longer effective as a campaigner. Ultimately, he became the object of the public's derision, viewed as a disreputable confidence man. Disgraced and in ill health, he was compelled to retire to a monastery in Leipzig.

In due course, a copy of Luther's 95 Theses reached Rome, and he was on the clerical hot seat. Numerous efforts to encourage him to recant regarding his views did nothing to alter his stance. Consequently, in 1521, Pope Leo X officially excommunicated Luther from the church.

Shortly thereafter, he still refused to recant regarding his opinions and writings at the Diet of Worms—not an odd item on a menu, but a formal assembly of the Holy Roman Empire, held in the city of Worms— before the Holy Roman Emperor, Charles V: "Unless I am convinced by Scripture and plain reason, I do not accept the authority of the popes and councils for they have contradicted each other—my conscience is captive to the Word of God. I cannot and I will not recant anything for to go against conscience is neither right nor safe. God help me. Amen." He stood his ground acknowledging that he faced certain martyrdom, and his friends and supporters understood this as well.

After Luther and his allies departed Worms, Charles V, who stood to lose income because indulgence money was shared with his secular government, issued an edict, labeling Luther an outlaw and a heretic who could be killed without legal consequence. Luther was the outspoken and defiant enemy number one.

A scheme was conceived to protect Martin Luther from certain death. Prince Frederick III, Elector of Saxony, or Frederick the Wise, masterminded Luther's friendly abduction and had him taken into isolation at the Wartburg Castle. Otherwise, most assuredly, Martin Luther would have been executed.

The articulate, talented, and bullheaded monk spent about ten months alone as a prisoner of his inviolable convictions. Isolated with his thoughts, Luther communicated with the outside world via letters and occasional personal visits. Among his notable accomplishments during his sequester, during his time of wrestling with the devil himself, Luther translated the New Testament into German, referencing Latin and Greek translations to ensure accuracy and authenticity, to impart a genuine theological interpretation. He believed in the importance of people understanding God's Word in their native language. This phenomenal feat took a mere eleven weeks, and it set the standard for the German language for generations to follow. Until then several German dialects were spoken; Luther's translation became the basis for a vernacular language, a step toward greater unification among the German people. Finally, everyday citizens could read and understand the Bible! This accomplishment syncs with Luther's belief that education is of paramount importance, especially for children, who should be prepared for a useful life by means of a practical education. He recognized that a common language and an educated populous are an asset to a civilized society. Christians who can read and research the Bible independent of clergy or academic scholars should be disposed to a more genuine and less superstitious faith…in theory, at least.

The idea of an educated and discerning population aligns with Luther's principle of a "priesthood of all believers," a core aspect of Protestantism.

Luther's time alone at the Wartburg Castle, according to him, was punctuated by numerous bouts with the devil (or perhaps more accurately, depression). There is still evidence of an ink stain on the wall (some claim it's been touched up to conform with the legend) where Luther allegedly hurled his ink well, aimed at the devil, who tortured him in the middle of the night.

Out of controversy and conflict—spurred by honest, well-intentioned criticism—an ecclesiastical revolution was birthed. Martin Luther defied church and government authority with the posting of his notorious, "scrap of paper." He grew to understand that his observations/criticisms would not be sensibly acknowledged by those in power nor would they be civilly discussed and debated. His actions challenged the status quo and jeopardized the easy, generous flow of money to the church; the two-sided coin of money and power was at risk of being stolen and fiery conflict ensued. With his actions, Martin Luther demonstrated that one person—determined, courageous, principled, educated, and smart—could impact an entrenched officialdom in critical need of reform, which is all he really wanted. He never set out to break away, to start a new church; he loved the church. Observing what he believed was corruption and abuse, Luther merely appealed for positive change. By questioning and challenging unethical practices and outdated traditions and beliefs, he triggered an enlightened era of critical thinking and Biblical interpretation. One bold and brash (often crass), outspoken man shifted the trajectory of history.

CHAPTER 21

Table Talk

Back at home, Maritza and David are sitting at the dining room table, drinking an ice-cold lemonade. It is late evening and summer's light is gradually dimming. As is the case most times these days, when they talk, it's either about the church or about Kyle. They begin with Kyle and the recent trouble at the recovery center.

"He's got such a temper sometimes," Maritza begins. "That guy, Marty, probably deserved to be knocked on his ass, but that's no excuse."

"And maybe Kyle should be more careful about picking a fight with someone more his size," observes David. "So foolish."

Maritza continues, "Thank God he's not being charged with anything. Marty has such a long rap sheet. Kyle's not been in any trouble before, so the police focused on Marty. He was high as a kite and could have killed Kyle...scary thought."

The detective informed them that Marty will face several charges, including aggravated assault. And based on his prior record, he'll probably do some serious jail time. Kyle should expect to be called as a witness when the time comes.

David laments, "Oy vey! Why did we want to have a kid anyway? What were we thinking? I really can't remember back that far. It's like so many decisions we make in life—if we knew exactly what the eventual outcome would be, we would never agree to it. Having kids is at the same time a most wonderful and terrible experience!"

Maritza responds, "Yeah, I'm with you on that. I was having second thoughts when I was in labor...thirty hours of excruciating pain, wondering when the heck this kid was gonna come out. While you conveniently discharged yourself to quite a few satisfying meals in the hospital dining hall."

David adds, "While you chomped on ice chips! Ha, a man's gotta eat, right?"

Maritza says, "At that point there was no turning back. We were in it for the long haul. I'm trying to remember what Martin Luther had to say about children."

"Here ya go again, getting analytical about Martin Luther!" David observes. "Okay, lay it on me. What did Doctor Luther have to say?"

Maritza refers to her library resource, *What Luther Says* (compiled by Ewald M. Plass):

> *God marvelously creates children and will provide for them. Why do you not daily learn the article of divine creation by looking at your children and offspring, who stand before you? They are of far greater worth than all the fruits of the trees. Here you may behold the providence of God, who created them out of nothing. In a half year, he gave them body and life and all their members and also intends to support them. But we pass by these gifts, nay, are bound to become blind and miserly because of them; for people usually are made worse and more covetous by the gift of children. They soon begin to pinch and do not know that every infant is given his lot in life ("fortuna"), according to the proverb: The greater the number of children, the greater the luck. Dear Lord God, how great are the ignorance and wickedness in man, who cannot consider these things, but acts contrary in his use of the best gifts of God.* (W-T 3, No. 3613—A. Lauterbach and J. Weller, June 18–July 28, 1537)

God himself must bless child training. It still happens to many parents that their children turn out to be bad, even when they have had good training. God does not want us to give them free rein and to grant them their will, but we are to train and teach them with all diligence. If our efforts are successful, we should thank God; if not, we have at least done our part. For that children turn out to be good does not lie in our power and might, but in God's. If he is not in the ship with us, we shall never sail smoothly. (W 24, 591 f—E 34, 224—SL 3, 529)

Love, like water, flows readily to lower levels, goes easily to those most in need of it; for as an emotion it is related to benevolence and sympathy. It is not surprising then that parental love is usually stronger than filial love.

David says, "Truthfully, it's been a mostly positive experience, having a child. But this is a particularly challenging time, isn't it?"

Maritza reacts, "Yeah, the glorious teenage years! Hard to believe we were teenagers once. Young and dumb."

David says, "Yeah, so long ago. Way back in the *nineteen hundreds!*"

David chuckles and then moves the conversation in another direction, "Speaking of old things from the nineteen hundreds, that organ at church is in dire need of repairs and restoration. Tom has said he has to do so many workarounds to play it somewhat effectively. It's very frustrating for him. He even has to limit the music repertoire because of its imperfections. And those damn cyphers are so distracting during the service…you never know when one is going to start whistling or screeching."

Maritza agrees, "Seems they happen right when I'm making the best points in my sermon. The punch of the message is totally lost because everyone is distracted! Assuming they are even listening, of course."

David adds, "Just hate when that happens! Kind of like a wailing kid, right?" He laughs. "Yesterday Tom spoke with the organ repair guy, and he thinks we're looking at a bill in the neighborhood of $125,000. The organ needs new leathering of pneumatic pouches and reservoirs, cleaning and repairing the pipes, tuning, chest replacement, and refinishing the console; it's a lot of work."

Maritza is astonished. "$125,000? Yowza! Where are we gonna find *that* kind of money? The church barely has enough money to pay the utility bills. We can't afford that big an expense! We should get the estimate in writing so I can take this up with church leadership. I'm sure we're going to want to look at alternatives. You know, many churches are moving away from the organ as the musical centerpiece. Maybe it's time for a change. Maybe we'll just sing everything *a cappella* like the Mennonites do, ha ha!"

Being a pipe organ buff, David thinks the pipe organ should be repaired, saving tradition and a shining example of innovative mechanical engineering. In the sixteenth century, many a European town held two objects in highest esteem—its clock and its church organ—both being premiere marvels of invention, sources of civic pride, and symbols of modern achievement.

"There are only a couple of alternatives, really," David offers. "We could look at an electronic organ or at having a praise band. Or we could just use piano accompaniment for worship. Have to say, I feel strongly that scrapping the old instrument would be like sentencing a beloved friend to the grave. And I think a lot of our parishioners would feel the same way."

Maritza says, "Music is such an important part of our ministry, our tradition. I certainly get that. We'll figure out a solution, one which people can live with and support."

David agrees, "Yeah, without music our worship services would be pretty anemic. What better way is there to enhance the spectrum of emotion expressed in the gospel than with music? It's kind of like adding a touch of theater to the message."

"I'm with you all the way on that," Maritza responds. "It's just that blasted money part that concerns me, like it always does. We'll have to figure it out."

"We will. We will," David ends the discussion. "Listen, I'm pretty beat, so I'm heading off to bed. Tomorrow's another busy day."

Maritza answers, "I'm going to stay up a bit longer to meditate and decompress. I'll be there in a few minutes. Sweet dreams!"

David mimics her, singing as he walks away, "Sweet dreams!"

Taking a couple of cleansing breaths, Maritza sits back, closes her eyes, and tries to clear her head. She has so many things going on right now, so many plates balanced on a stick, that it's a challenge to relax. Sometimes she feels like a thousand streaking comets—thoughts, events, and problems—are flashing across her consciousness simultaneously. It's no wonder her sleep is often fitful and interrupted.

After a couple minutes of focusing on her breathing...slow, easy, deep...she drifts into a dreamy, meditative state. She prays for peace, for clarity. This art of faraway centering, of spiritual connection, has been such a helpful skill, not taught in seminary. She has found value in the heretical Gospel of Thomas, which holds the idea of the kingdom being inside you *and* outside you. In these quiet moments with her eyes shut, she looks for the light within.

Gradually, she perceives a presence at the table where David had been sitting.

Slightly puzzled, she thinks, *Has David come back to talk some more? Wait, no, is this an angel? Or it might be the devil! Maybe if I sing, he'll go away.* She hums her favorite hymn, "Amazing Grace," at a somewhat faster tempo than usual. Her apprehension increases. She doesn't dare open her eyes.

A baritone voice joins in. Startled, Maritza continues humming, curiously afraid to stop, as she realizes her singing partner is *not David.* The singing duet cadences with a *ritardando* as Maritza thinks about the text while humming—"Was blind, but now I see."

She looks up and exclaims, "Dear God in heaven, what is this? *Who is this?* I must be losing my mind! Are you evil or good? It feels like you might be Lucifer. Are you Lucifer?"

The mysterious specter responds, "No, Luther...Lu-*ther!*" He thinks, *Why does everyone think I'm Lucifer? So annoying!*

Confused and yet a bit relieved, Maritza confirms, "Luther? *The Martin Luther?*"

"Yes, yes, yes, Martin Luther!"

Shaking her head, Maritza asks, "What in the world *is* this? What are *you* doing here? You have a lovely singing voice, by the way."

Appreciating the compliment, Luther replies, "Why thank you! You as well. You should sing in the choir."

"What?" Maritza asks. "Wait, wait, wait. Let's not get off topic here. Tell me why you're here. Why have you invaded my quiet time? What's going on here exactly?"

Luther explains, "You've opened your heart and mind, praying for a sense of clarity and understanding. I'm here to help enlighten you, as one who has learned much by questioning, analyzing, and experiencing."

"So God *does* answer prayer!" Maritza concludes. "Imagine that! Not quite the answer I was expecting, but as the saying goes, 'The good Lord works in mysterious ways!'"

Luther continues, "It might seem like an odd place to begin, but why don't we start by talking about that broken-down musical instrument in your church? What Mozart called 'the King of Instruments.' The King is stumbling off his throne, methinks."

"He's a royal pain!" Maritza exclaims. "We've gotten a lot of mileage out of that dear beloved friend, but we are at a tipping point…should we ditch it? Repair it or replace it? Why does everything have to cost so much?"

Luther responds, "Money is a constant worry, isn't it? My dear Katie was skillful at stretching our financial resources. Thank goodness, because I had no interest or ability in that area. What I *can* advise you on is the importance of preserving musical tradition, of maintaining music as a means of heavenly expression. The beautiful thing about the organ is that it can be played loud enough to support congregational singing, and it can be played softly and delicately to create a mood for meditation and reflection. It has a wonderful and wide color spectrum. In effect, it replicates an orchestra. As long as you can find someone to play it!"

Maritza agrees. "Yes, we are so blessed to have Tom as our organist. I hope he never decides to retire!"

"Maybe you can find a way to combine the old and the new," Luther offers. "Isn't there new technology in your modern era which, for less money than a pipe organ, can combine traditional features and new musical options? Surely, there must be."

Maritza responds, "We'll have to research it some more. No matter what, it's going to be a challenging leap of faith for our church. Our finances aren't so great. We're probably going to need a new roof soon as well."

Offering encouragement, Luther responds, "You know, sometimes when challenges like this arise, it gives a church and its people something to focus on, something to rally behind. When there's no purposefulness, a congregation can grow stale, even stagnate. Initially, this may seem like a roadblock, but it just might be an opportunity instead...a chance for people to unite behind a common effort. I would surmise that your flock will do whatever it takes to maintain its musical identity and heritage."

"I'm sure you're right," Maritza agrees. "We Lutherans are not called 'the singing church' for nothing! We treasure our music and value its power; there's no doubt about it. We have such a rich history of superb music, including that of Johann Sebastian Bach, the so-called Father of Music. He was so prolific and inventive; his sacred works are exquisite, divinely expressive."

Luther says, "Would that I could have written music as beautiful as he did. Such a gifted musician!" Then he reflectively quotes himself, "Beautiful music is the art of the prophets that can calm the agitations of the soul; it is one of the most magnificent and delightful presents God has given us."

"That sounds like a notable quote," Maritza observes. "Where'd that originate?"

Luther says slyly, "I'll never tell!"

Maritza pleads, "Really? Come on! What other pearls of wisdom do you have?"

"How about, 'Next to the word of God, the noble art of music is the greatest treasure in the world.'"

Maritza smiles. "I like it! Let me write that down. 'Next to the word of God...' I'm sure you have more."

Luther says, "Let me think. How about this regarding some people's tendency to be critical just for the sake of being critical? Seems there's always a nitpicker, a smug know-it-all. 'Criticizing is easy work. The spectator (Master Wiseacre) can play the game best. For he imagines that if he were to get the (bowling) ball into his hands, he would hit twelve pins, although only nine are standing on the alley. So they imagine until they find out that there is also a gutter running alongside the alley.'"

Maritza adds, "Sounds like what we refer to as the 'devil's advocate.' And speaking of the devil, I know you have an awful lot to say about him."

Luther admits, "Hoo boy, don't get me started! Where to begin? Let me see now…there is so much I could say. How about let's start with this?

"A popular proverb posits that, 'Where God builds a church, the devil builds a tavern next door.' And people used to tell this fable: 'When God made man out of a clod of earth and breathed into his nostrils the breath of life so that man became a living soul, the devil wanted to imitate God and also took a clod of earth in order to make a man of it; but it turned out to be a toad!' The message is that the devil is always the imitator of our Lord God, forever posing as divine and creates the impression that he is God.

"The great imitator, the vile deceiver, loiters on the fringes, looking for an opening to make empty assurances, to hoodwink, capitalizing on vulnerable souls' fear and selfishness. Just as Satan tried to tempt Jesus as he walked alone in the wilderness for forty days, he tests us day and night. It is only natural to want to follow an easy path, to open the door, to surrender to the devil's false promises. The divine Word, as found in the Bible, is our fortress against the great deceiver, Satan."

Maritza observes, "This is really good material. Mind if I use it in my sermon?"

Luther answers, "Sure, absolutely fine."

"But I don't think I'll say that Martin Luther told me to tell you..." Maritza concludes.

Luther agrees. "Indeed, people will think you're under the influence!"

Maritza asks, "So about the Bible...there's a lot of material there, a lot to digest, to analyze and understand. If it's misinterpreted, passages taken out of context, it can be misused and even exploited, no?"

Luther agrees, "Yes, of course, that's right."

Maritza continues, "And what about the fact that certain *men* decided throughout the centuries what material would be and what would *not* be included in the Bible? Is the Good Book as we know it the whole story?"

Luther answers, "Well, I don't think the book, the Bible, itself will ever be altered, but there is a lot more to the 'story.' That much is clear. Here is a fundamentally important point to remember: God and his Word are constant, never changing. To illustrate, the foundation of a substantial building never changes, although the building's layout, design, and décor may be altered over time. The building's support structure remains firm."

Maritza adds, "How firm a foundation!"

Luther agrees, "And *a mighty fortress!*"

Maritza says, "There should really be a song written on that subject!"

Luther smiles and agrees, "That would be wonderful, wouldn't it?"

"So on the subject of interpretation, the message one gleans from Scripture depends on what one concludes about the truth. And that can be a thorny pursuit sometimes," Maritza says.

Luther agrees, "Yes, that is certainly true. Even the villain Pontius Pilate recognized that truth can mean very different things to different people. But let's not treat him as an authority on truth. Everyone must take care to be certain of the true doctrine by himself/ herself and must not base his/her convictions solely on what other people have concluded. Likewise, 'do not make articles of faith from your *own* thoughts, lest your faith become but a dream.'"

"Let me make sure I'm getting this right," Maritza says. "In other words, don't take truth for granted, based on what others tell you. Draw your own conclusions but base them on God's word and on your own logical judgment. This sounds a bit contradictory, doesn't it? God's word is firm, but everyone can have their own idea about what is truth?"

Luther answers, "Yes, it is a bit tricky. It can take a lifetime of study and prayer to grow in faith and understanding. Bear in mind that truth is not a finite commodity; it is an infinitely flowing well-spring which can never be exhausted. 'As for me, my eyes are directed to nothing but the cause of the truth as such. This I heartily love! In case I am, or at times were to be, too free and forceful in the interest of this cause, I desire everybody kindly to forgive me the offense. I do not know what I can do beyond this. God's will be done on earth as it is in heaven. Amen.'"

Maritza pauses, then says, "Amen!"

Wanting to take full advantage of this opportunity to interview the great doctor, she asks, "Apart from truth, I want to ask you about the whole 'good works versus grace' idea. I think I get it, but what would you say about that?"

Luther responds, "Yes, that's a really important topic, for sure. I spent years and years trying to perfectly adhere to God's command- ments (not surprising, given my background in civil law), and finally it hit me—God is not a disciplinarian or a jailer or a judge. Very simply, *God is love!* He loves me and everyone else because he is the Creator. Just as a parent wants a child to grow up to be fulfilled, successful, compassionate, and loving, God desires what is best for us, his creation. His love and grace are free for the claiming once we recognize that we need them. When I finally washed away all the clutter of human-created rules, prerequisites, academic doctrines, and *guilt*—that's a really big one, by the way—I had this epiphany! It was this euphoric 'aha' moment when I felt like running wildly down the street hollering at the top of my lungs, 'I've got the most amazing news! Accept God's grace…it's *free!*' Talk about good news! The glory of grace is to be highly praised, and it cannot be praised highly enough. As Paul exclaims in 2 Corinthians, 'Thanks be unto God for his unspeakable gift!'"

Maritza adds, "Such a great way of explaining it! A wonderful gift! Brings tears of joy to my eyes. Truly, this is the most liberating concept. It is the key to the door of redemption for anyone—for the prisoner, the thief, the liar, the addict…even for the murderer. Although I admit that last one is a tall order."

"It is," agrees Luther. "But remember who stands out among the New Testament penmen. Who was the wisest man after Christ?"

Maritza answers, "That would have to be Saint Paul, also known as 'Saul of Tarsus.'"

"Correct! And what did he do *before* his conversion on the road to Damascus?"

"He persecuted Christians," Maritza answers. "Some to the point of martyrdom. He was apparently ruthless in his pursuit of Christian believers.

"And while he was traveling with companions to Damascus where Christian beliefs were beginning to grow, he was struck by a light so bright that it blinded him and he fell to the ground. A voice asked him, 'Saul, Saul, why are you persecuting me?'

"Paul asked, 'Who are you?'

"The voice replied, 'I am Jesus, the one whom you are persecuting. Go into the city and you will be told what to do.'"

Luther chimes in, "And we both know the rest of the story. Upon his 'conversion,' Paul became the greatest Christian evangelist of all time! His letters comprise a majority of the New Testament. He, of all people, was the 'chosen vessel' who traveled to many foreign lands, spreading the good news about the Messiah. As you know, he spent a few years-long stints in prison for his determination and defiance; ultimately, he was executed (beheaded) under the Roman Emperor Nero around AD 67."

"A sad and inauspicious end for such a good, noble, and holy person," Maritza says.

"Here is *the* great example," Luther continues, "of the ultimate redemption, by the grace of God. If Saul of Tarsus could be redeemed, certainly anyone can be—and that includes you and me. Notice that he is remembered more for the many good things that he did, and not for the evil he committed earlier in his life."

"That example," Maritza concludes, "should be inspiring to anyone who is looking for redemption and hope. I suppose even for a murderer, but that's *still* problematic for me, I must confess."

Luther agrees, "Some things are best left in God's hands."

Maritza asks, "So how would you sum up this controversial idea of not earning salvation by doing good works? You know that some naysayers will point out that, if we don't earn eternal life by doing good deeds, then what's the point in even doing them?"

Luther answers without hesitation, "God does not need our good works, but our neighbor does."

"I like it!" Maritza says. She continues, "But what about the law? Certainly, we still need the law."

"Obedience to God's law," Luther explains, "is protection from destruction, but not necessarily from God himself. God is not looking to punish us if we don't abide by the law. Like a parent would instruct her children to stay on a positive and virtuous path to avoid unnecessary pain and disappointment, so God wants us to stay on a path which is in sync with his divine will. Law is critically important and necessary for civilization. Otherwise, no one would have a conscience, and there would be chaos. I firmly assert, as Paul did, that the law (e.g. the Ten Commandments, religious practices, moral standards, etc.) and the gospel are both God's Word. However, understand this basic doctrine: *the law demands, and the Gospel gives.* There is the distinct and meaningful difference. This idea is manifested in the Book of John: 'For God sent not his son into the world to condemn the world, but that the world through him might be saved.'"

Maritza is somewhat awestruck. "That is so incredibly powerful! I see what you mean. I am definitely going to think on these concepts and discuss them at my church."

Luther nods and says, "That's really great!"

Maritza says, "I am so enjoying this conversation; you have no idea! I'm sure there are a thousand more things we should talk about, but—"

"But my time is limited," Luther interrupts. "And I don't want to give you too many answers because you might stop searching. That wouldn't be good."

"Understood," Maritza concedes. "Okay, so what would you say is your final word of advice?"

Luther turns his head skyward, lifts his eyebrows, and thoughtfully says, "I would say, seek and speak the truth…and try not to be anxious. Trust in God, and don't be afraid."

"That's wonderful, thank you!" Maritza says. "Could we possibly conclude by reciting Psalm 150 as a call and response? I think that would be a beautiful way to bring our conversation to a close."

Luther responds, "Sure, why not? I think I remember this one. You begin."

Praise the LORD! *Praise God in his sanctuary; praise him in his mighty firmament!*

Praise him for his mighty deeds; praise him according to his exceeding greatness!

Praise him with trumpet sound; praise him with lute and harp!

Praise him with timbrel and dance; praise him with strings and pipe!

Praise him with sounding cymbals; praise him with loud clashing cymbals!

Let everything that breathes praise the LORD! *Praise the* LORD!

Maritza repeats, "Praise the LORD!"

Luther says, "I must go now. Grace and peace to you!"

Maritza repeats, "Grace and peace to you. Thank you, Martin Luther! Thank you!"

The great Doctor Luther's image melts away into the dimness of nightfall.

Feeling a bit unsteady and trying to be as quiet as she can be, Maritza rises and shuffles off to bed. She thinks, *How in the world am I ever going to get to sleep after that?*

CHAPTER 22

———————

The Imprisoned, the Poor, the Needy

The next day, Maritza rises early, which is her usual pattern. She realizes that she forgot to prepare the coffee the night before; normally she sets the timer for 5:00 a.m. so the coffee is already brewed when she hazily stumbles from the bedroom to the kitchen at 5:30. The scintillating aroma of java normally permeates the whole house and nudges her to get moving, to face the new day. Oh well. She can excuse her forgetfulness because she was distracted by her most amazing conversation with the mysterious and fantastic visitor last night. To have had the privilege of a give-and-take with the great reformer, Martin Luther, is an experience she'll never forget. As she's preparing the freshly ground coffee—her beloved daily caffeine infusion—she thinks she *must* put this experience in writing. She tells herself, *Once the fog is lifted, get to the computer and write this all out. I don't want to forget a single word of what he said. Some might think a spiritual encounter such as this is a hallucination, but it sure seemed real. Why would it not be? The Bible contains many instances where mortals and spiritual messengers intersect.*

"Whether this experience was real or imagined, I'm going to take Luther's messages to heart, because it just makes sense to do so." She states with absolute assurance, "I will seek and speak the truth, and do it fearlessly." She pauses for a moment. "But I don't think I should tell David about my experience, at least not yet. He'll think I'm quite crazy."

Maritza is gazing out the window, lost in thought, when David walks into the kitchen to grab his coffee. Knowing the answer will be about the same each morning, he asks, "So how'd you sleep?"

"Oh, pretty well, once I *got* to sleep," Maritza answers. "I had some pretty vivid and detailed dreams, but they were very good dreams, thankfully."

Almost as though he didn't really hear what she said, he replies, "Hmm, that's nice." Then he exits the kitchen toward the living room to catch up on the news on his computer.

She thinks, *At least he didn't probe me for more information. That's a blessing.*

After warming her coffee with a top-off, she walks to her study to start typing, to make a record of her profound and provocative exchange with the venerable Doctor Luther.

Two hours of focused recollection and speedy typing ensue. Feeling like she's making really good progress, she is startled out of her recall zone with the ping of a text message: "Please contact the church office ASAP!" The parish secretary, Lisa, always texts her rather than calling, just in case she's in a meeting or otherwise indisposed.

Maritza thinks, "Sounds like it's a crisis, but it's probably nothing. She probably wants to know if the property committee has been informed about the broken stained-glass window in the sanctuary. What kind of person vandalizes a church anyway? Better check in to see what's going on."

Lisa answers the phone, "St. Paul's Lutheran Church."

Maritza says, "Hey, Lisa! You asked me to call?"

Lisa explains, "Yes, the people from the prison ministry just called and said they urgently need volunteers. Some people dropped out after the Rabbi Lamm situation. Do we have anyone who would be willing to help by spearheading a Bible study group or by leading a worship service? The Bible study is on Tuesday nights, and the worship service is on Friday nights. There would be a training/certification process so the individuals would be well prepared for this special ministry. Shall we put something in the bulletin?"

Maritza answers, "No, I don't think we should do an all call for this type of thing. I think I'll speak directly with a couple key people so we find just the right person or persons for this important task. I have some specific individuals in mind already."

"Okay, that's fine," answers Lisa. "Just let me know if you need me to do anything else."

"Just leave the contact information for me in my inbox," Maritza says. "Thanks so much!" She hangs up.

As she turns to resume formulating her Luther revelation, she thinks this prison outreach could be a good opportunity to expand her church's mission. They've done so many other things to help those in need, but never participated in prison ministry. Most would acknowledge this seems like a necessary and important mission, but it would probably be a scary prospect for most of her church members. It must be just the right fit for one or two people at first.

She ponders, *Hmm...DAVID! He would be perfect! And maybe Mike Goodman too! They could even alternate every other week; they'd make a strong team, I think! David's been hinting that he'd like to find a new way to enrich his spiritual life, maybe help others in a new direction. And Mike sure could use something to focus on, to take his mind off his family tragedy. I'll approach them both separately, maybe tell each that the other has already committed. Nah, too sneaky. I'll play it straight. If it's meant to be, they'll agree to do it, at least for a while. After all, it's not a life sentence!*

So where was I? Maritza asks herself. *Oh, yes. Grace versus works. It's fascinating and at the same time puzzling how this concept of grace is so misunderstood, or not grasped at all. Its healing, rejuvenating message is crowded out by so many other categorically useless things.*

She thinks further, *I'm sorry I didn't get a chance to go deeper with Luther on the subject of helping the poor and needy, lifting up the downtrodden. We touched on it when he talked about how God does not need our good deeds, but our neighbor does. His answer was so simple and to the point. I know Luther ministered to many disadvantaged and broken individuals, even comforting people afflicted with disease while disregarding his own well-being. To a casual observer, Luther might have given the impression, especially later in life, of a crusty, cranky curmudgeon, but his compassion for others was evident in his frequently altruistic behavior.*

She refers to her personal library on this subject. Luther's view is evident in his words: "Do not think that the world is bound to recognize our good works or to let them be uncriticized. A Christian must act like a good apple tree, which offers and displays its fruits to everyone and even distributes them among the swine and the bad beasts that tear at its roots."

Furthermore, he advised Christians not to expect gratitude: "Among Christians, where one wants to help the other, this should be done with singleness of purpose so that nothing is sought but the honor of God and the benefiting of our neighbor, without noting whether he is grateful. The heart should say: I do it gladly, willingly, and take delight in it; let a man react however he pleases. God, too, gives many things in vain and expects nothing in return."

She analyzes, "In the Book of Matthew, Jesus in fact said it best when he talked about the Son of Man, in his glory and on his throne, acknowledging the righteous who asked him, 'Lord, when did we see you hungry and feed you, or thirsty and give you something to drink? When did we see you a stranger and invite you in, or needing clothes and clothe you? When did we see you sick or in prison and go to visit you?'

"The King will reply, 'Truly I tell you, whatever you did for the least of these my brothers and sisters of mine, you did for me.'

"This could be interpreted to mean helping the needy gets you 'atta boys' in the afterlife, but I think it's more selfless than that. Helping the most vulnerable—the hungry, the thirsty, the naked, the sick, the imprisoned—is what the great physician did, and we should follow his example."

Sensing the pressure to wrap up this "conversation with myself" and get on with her day, Maritza saves her notes as "MartinLutherDoc" on the computer and gets ready to head into the church office.

CHAPTER 23

A Change of Heart

Kyle comes hurtling down the stairs, sounding like a stampeding herd of wildebeests. "Mom, can you drop me at school on your way to the church?"

Maritza thinks he'll break his neck on those stairs one of these days and says, "Wait, didn't the doctor say you should stay home a couple of days to make sure you're okay? You shouldn't jump back in the race too soon."

"I'm fine," Kyle says. "Besides, I'd be bored out of my mind staying home. I really want to go to class."

"All right then," Maritza concedes. She ponders, *Wonder what's gotten into him? Sounds like he's anxious to hit the books. Maybe that concussion shook loose the common-sense reservoir in his brain. Whatever it is, let's just roll with it.*

In the car, mother and son have a wide-ranging and meaningful conversation. Maritza is amazed; it's almost like Kyle is a different person!

She can't help herself, so she asks, "Are you okay? I mean, you seem really jazzed today, which is a good thing, of course. I'm pleased that you seem energized and positive…you're not taking that 5-hour ENERGY stuff, are you?"

Kyle laughs. "No, I'm just high on life. That's how you want me to be, isn't it?"

Maritza responds, "Of course! Just making sure yours is a natural high. Sorry if I seem suspicious. You know me, the 'worrier-in-chief.'"

"Stop worrying, Mom! I know I'm going to be okay, and you shouldn't doubt that either. You know, your anxiety about me isn't exactly a confidence builder. Do you think that God worries about you?"

"Ooo, ouch!" Maritza takes the verbal bullet in stride. "Ya know, that's a very good question. I don't think God even experiences worry. That just seems contrary to the very nature of God, doesn't it? You make a very good point for someone so young and so green, I have to say. How'd you get to be so doggone smart?"

"The apple doesn't fall too far from the tree!" Kyle answers.

"Now that's delicious!" Maritza thinks.

Kyle says, "Ya know, Mom; I was thinking, I want to research what it would take to be a counselor, a therapist. What courses would I need? How long would it take, and how much would it cost?"

Maritza is dumbfounded! She thinks, *Geez Louise, he is actually starting to sound like an adult! His dad and I have wanted him to go to college, but only if he had some idea of a specific course of study. No sense going off to an expensive school, spending all that tuition money, not having an eventual vocation in mind.*

Wanting to sound thoughtful and not too euphoric, Maritza says, "Why don't you do some research on your own, speak with your guidance counselor? In the meantime, I'll speak with a couple of my colleagues to find out what their certification process has been. Then we can compare notes. Sound good?"

Kyle says, "Sounds great! I feel like I want to do something to make a difference, to help others. I'm sure it will be a challenging process, to become a counselor, but I think this is something I can really sink my teeth into. I'm also sure working with broken people will have its frustrations; I won't make much money, but that's okay. Hopefully, my life will be enriched in other ways."

Maritza's response chokes in her throat. With tears welling up, in a quivering voice she utters, "That sounds just wonderful, son. Really...wonderful!"

They arrive at the school, and Maritza pulls up to the curb. Kyle opens the car door and bounds away like an enthusiastic, buoyant five-year-old. "Bye, Mom! Have a super-dooper day!"

She hollers, "Have a great day, you goofball!" Then she says to herself, *What the heck's gotten into that kid?*

As she drives on to the church, she is filled with wonder, thinking what a blessing a family can be. She and David have provided a life and a foundation for this prodigal son. Maybe he has wandered sufficiently off the path that he understands what a valuable and trustworthy refuge the family unit is, how important and powerful love is. Maybe the light of love has broken through the hard barrier of adolescent selfishness. Who can explain it?

CHAPTER 24

Unhinged, Through the Prison Gate

Six years later...

Alone in the dank and miserable prison cell, Marty sits on the edge of the bed and thinks back on the events that led to his incarceration. The newer charges of drug trafficking and aggravated assault, combined with his previous record, could have led to longer jail time; he figures he was probably lucky to get a six-year sentence. It could have been worse; his attorney did a pretty good job. Every day he dreams of the moment he can confront Kyle and hurt him, terrorize him. And Carla too. They've got to pay for the misery they've caused. Maybe they'll even pay the ultimate price! He carefully considers his torturous options. His opportunity for revenge is nearly at hand; his release date is just around the bend. It's only a matter of days.

He thinks, *Gotta be strategic about this, lay out my plan.*

During his stay at the "purgatory penitentiary," as he and some of his cellmates affectionately call it, Marty has been unable to focus on anything other than getting his perfect revenge. His cancerous mindset has metastasized over these six years; he has pushed away any thoughts of getting his life on a positive track. Many have shown their concern for him. The prison chaplain has tried to help him, a church-based prison ministry has tried, a Bible study group organized by other "residents" has tried. Despite his flagrant rudeness and closed-minded attitude, even a pair of Jehovah's Witnesses have repeatedly called on him, attempting to convert him. He admires their tenacity, but the JW take on religion is that of an authoritarian and punishing God—a God who does not tolerate disobedience or sinfulness. To put it bluntly, their preaching of God's judgment and angry retribution has about the same chance of winning him over as the Catholic Church would have of making him a priest. Ain't gonna happen…no way, no how!

Marty reflects, *I can't help but wonder what could possibly motivate these delusional jokers to keep knocking on my door to try to save me. No way I'm buyin' whatever BS they're sellin'. I'm so far gone, so far off the path, there's no one who can pull me back from the brink.*

Even the inhospitable reality of prison life hasn't brought Marty any closer to redemption. Seems he is destined to be drawn downstream toward the putrid wastepipe of self-destruction.

As his release date draws closer, Marty receives a message from the warden's office via the corrections officer. Bob Weiss, the drug counselor he knows from DARC, wants to visit him the next morning at ten o'clock.

At first, he says, "No way! After all this time, he shows up? Why should I agree to meet with him?"

The corrections officer replies, "He wants to be sure to check in with you before you transition to life on the outside. He wants to make sure you're ready and that you have access to what you need. Here is someone who cares what happens to you. You should talk to him."

Remembering Bob's always genuine concern for people like himself, he reconsiders his response. "Okay, why not?" he answers, and thinks, *Bob has always been pretty tough on me, but he's always been real. Suppose it can't hurt to hear what Bob has to say.* He thinks back to the monotonous group counseling sessions which he was required to attend as a condition of his prior parole. *That was such torture! But I will say that Bob's personal story, which he told on several occasions, is admirable. How could someone become a highly respected, caring, and effective counselor after having sunk to such depths of hopelessness? It is a remarkable story. How did he do it? Why did he do it? I don't think I could ever do what he did.*

The next day, Bob arrives ten minutes early and waits for Marty to be brought into the meeting area. Finally, a corrections officer leads Marty to the table where Bob is seated; his hands are restrained in front by handcuffs. They share cautious, low-key hellos, and Bob asks Marty how he's doing.

"Doin' okay, I guess," Marty responds. "Looking forward to getting outta this hellhole. Can't be soon enough. What brings you here on this auspicious occasion? I've not seen or heard from you these six years, and *now* you come to see me?" He jokes, "Have you been on vacation this whole time?"

Bob explains, "I'm so sorry I've not been more available for you. My work at the recovery center has been overwhelming. We have so many patients we're bursting at the seams. We're having to turn some people away, referring them to other programs, which I'd rather not be doing. We just can't handle it all. I'm sure you can appreciate that this disease of addiction is spreading like crazy. It's like a highly contagious virus with no easy cure."

Marty says, "Yeah, I get it. Believe me, I get it."

"Has anyone from your family been visiting you and talking with you?" Bob asks. "I hope you've had some support from family or from a friend."

Marty conveniently forgets all of those who have tried to be helpful. "Nope. No one gives two stinkin' shits about me. I doubt there's anyone who cares whether I live or die, to be honest."

Bob says, "Well, that's very sad. Hard to believe, but very sad, yes. You know this is not an uncommon situation among addicts, right? No matter how much people may love someone—an addict—they often turn their backs on them after repeated disappointments. After betrayal and deceit...and many, many lies."

"I get that," Marty responds. "But I don't even have anyone to disappoint! My whole family is pretty much dead and gone. Except my brother, who is just gone; he could be dead for all I know. I haven't spoken to him or heard from him in years. My parents are deceased and so is my sister. *(Pauses)* Ah, my dear sister. If she were alive, things would be so different."

Bob asks, "How's that? In what way?"

Marty ponders, "Well, if I had been paying attention to what she was doing, when we were on a family vacation years ago."

Bob says, "Go on. What happened?"

Marty gets choked up, holding back his emotions.

"My family was vacationing in Canada, not far across the US-Canadian border. I was fishing off a dock by the cabin where we were staying. I loved to fish; I was twelve years old. I was so engrossed in what I was doing, I didn't notice my eight-year-old sister, Tabitha, skipping out on a dock about fifty feet from where I was. The dock she was on was partially submerged farther out where the water was deep. I think she slipped on the moss which built up where the dock tipped into the water. I noticed some commotion to my left, but at the same time, I felt a sharp pull on my fishing pole. Holy cow, I got a big one on the line! So I'm focusing on reeling in this fish, and I hear gasping and frantic splashing.

"I was so preoccupied with my prize catch, by the time I realized what was happening, it was too late. Precious seconds passed while I attended to my fish rather than looking after my sister. My brother Mark yelled to me to alert our parents as he tried to grab Tabitha to pull her out of the water. She didn't know how to swim and sank rapidly into the greenish water with her long hair spreading out like thick seaweed beneath the water's surface.

"My dad was roused from his nap and came running. He managed to bring her up out of the water onto the dock but was unable to revive her. We all stood around in utter shock and horror as we became aware of the terrible reality of the situation. My mom ran up to us on the dock with a look of complete and utter terror on her face. I'll never forget that. She was hysterical.

"Since that horrible, fateful day, I have lived with the crushing guilt of having let my sister die. Because I was so focused on my own selfish act, my innocent, beautiful sister died at eight years of age. The aftermath of that painful day was the gradual destruction of our family and of my parents. They were consumed with grief and sorrow, and both turned to alcohol to dull the pain. My dad was impossible to live with, beating us boys for the most minor infractions, sometimes with his leather belt. When I turned eighteen, my parents divorced. Mark and I moved out on our own to escape the madness. My dad died about ten years ago, from liver disease, and my mom eight years ago from cancer. I have never forgiven myself. We would have been a perfectly happy family if this had never happened. So maybe now you can understand a little of why I am the way I am. I live with an enormous shit pile of shame, regret, and self-hate. I need to escape this nightmare, so I turn to drugs. I just can't help it."

Bob observes, "That is a heartbreaking story, there's no doubt about that. If only things had turned out differently. If only. I feel very badly for you, Marty; I really do. The pain you've withstood all these years has been devastating. (*Pauses*) May I share an observation with you?"

Marty shirks, "Sure, go ahead."

Bob answers, "I've spent hours with you in group therapy, and you have never shared this story. Plus, you have just now articulated your experience and your feelings with such clarity, it's almost like you're a different person than the one I've known. Would you say you feel differently now compared to the time before you were incarcerated?"

Marty muses, "Maaay-bee?"

Bob continues, "I think the fact that you're not self-medicating has made you more clear-headed, more in touch with rational thinking and with your emotions. What do you think?"

Marty confesses, "I suppose I'm able to be a little clearer, but I'm still effed up. The only reason I'm sober now is because I can't get drugs here...surprise, surprise! To be honest, I've been looking forward to getting doped up. I think I deserve a little reward after six years."

Bob shakes his head. "This is why I wanted to see you now before you get out again. The fact that you've been sober for a long time could be an opportunity for you to stay sober, to get your life on a good path. I know the correctional system offers programs to help former inmates transition back into society, and I would encourage you to take advantage of those. I would also suggest you contact me right away when you are able to do so, to put a program in place whereby I can help you. You know how to reach me. Promise me we'll meet up soon."

Somewhat reluctantly, Marty answers, "Sure, I guess so." He presses his lips and concludes, "I'll call ya."

Bob is not entirely convinced of Marty's sincerity. He thinks at least he has offered help; he knows that's all he can ever do. Marty's festering guilt over his sister's death, his belief that his inaction allowed her to die, has corroded his soul. Is redemption and healing even possible for someone like Marty, whose condition is so thoroughly imbedded? Pretty incredible how one incident—one which occurred in a matter of minutes—could impact the complexion of one's life for years and years to come. It's incredibly tragic and heartbreaking. So sad.

He makes a mental note to be sure to alert Kyle to the fact that Marty is being released from prison. He and his family should be vigilant.

CHAPTER 25

Practically in Love

For the officially joined, legally certified, well-matched twosome, it's been a refreshing and relaxing couple of weeks since the *big wedding*. Not an extravagant event, the quite beautiful reception was preceded by a traditional religious ceremony. Kyle and Carla intentionally planned a somewhat modest celebration, with a limited number of guests, to keep costs down. Saving for a down payment on a house rather than spending the equivalent of King Croesus' fortune on an elaborate party seemed so much more sensible. Hopefully, the uninvited peripheral friends and distant relatives weren't too upset about not having been invited. Oh well, can't please everyone. Kyle, ever the pragmatist, thinks weddings are really more of a civil matter than a religious one, but for the sake of familial accord, he agreed to a religious observance. Weddings have become big business, and the splashier the event the more likely the marriage won't last, so Carla says anyway. Besides, leaning on their parents to underwrite a huge wedding just didn't seem right. They have become frugal to a fault, so spending big money on a single day celebration would go against their natures, no question about it.

Through the college years, Kyle and Carla have hustled, sacrificed, borrowed, and economized; they've survived by being exceedingly cost-conscious, often drawing sustenance from ramen noodles, chipped bacon, and Doritos. At least their taste buds were gratified as they adhered to their "salt of the earth" diet. There has been an occasional lettuce salad to appease Mother Maritza's sermonizing about eating better. Bacon and cheese always boosted a boring salad to a peak level of enjoyment, especially with store-brand blue cheese dressing slathered on. Hamburger Helper—a bachelor's savory delight—was a handy stay-at-home treat…quick, cheap, and tasty. And for a special spontaneous extravagance, they would split a delicious cheese steak hoagie with raw onions, tomatoes, oregano, and just a little bit of mayo! Being that they were constantly on the go, well-planned, healthy, and nutritious meals just were not realistic.

Now that they've earned master's degrees and tied the conjugal knot, the moment has arrived to look intelligent and get serious about many important aspects of their lives—nutrition, exercise, relationships, employment. Time to put away childish things, to be an adult and to be responsible for heaven's sake! (Mother Maritza might wax philosophical and say it's high time for them to *become* the salt of the earth rather than simply *consuming* it!) Important milestones have been achieved, and now new dreams and goals will gradually come into focus. It's an exciting and critical phase whereby the joyously united couple will define their promising future together. Might children be in the mix someday? Time will tell.

*****

Katharina von Bora was the former Benedictine nun who became Martin Luther's devoted wife, household manager, child-rearer, confidante, and consultant. He referred to her by several names—"the Boss of Zulsdorf," "My Lord, Katie," "Lutheress," and "the Morning Star of Wittenberg" for her pattern of rising at 4:00 a.m. to attend to her many household duties.

The Luthers' marriage was foundationally important, not only for them personally, but also for the larger cause of the reformation movement. Their relationship—and their home, family, friends, and a devoted community of believers—provided a framework of support and inspiration. Essentially, without the many good-hearted, well-meaning, and trustworthy supporters around him, including his beloved wife and family, Luther might never have had such an extensive impact on the dispirited world around him. A truth-seeking community of the faithful—both near and far—was the interlaced societal network through which Luther's philosophy, theology and groundbreaking ideas were circulated.

Imagine if history had instead been that Luther's posting of the 95 Theses resulted in his immediate execution. A reformation movement probably would have occurred much later, and it would have unfolded very differently. Without Luther, the community of believers would have been like sheep without a shepherd, not knowing which direction to go. And without her husband Martin and his writings, Katharina would have remained a nun her entire life, deprived of the joy and richness of family life...denied the mixed blessing of being a pastor's wife!

The Luthers' union was a curious liaison, an unbelievable intersection reached via a crooked and improbable road.

Katharina was born into an impoverished noble family. Because she had no dowry, she faced two possible destinations in life—either she could be a nun, or she would become a spinster. Because Katharina's mother had recently died, her father sent her at age five to the convent school of the Benedictine cloister in Brehna to receive a formal education. When she was nine years old, she was moved to the convent of Nimbschen, where, subsequently, at age sixteen, she dutifully took a vow of silence, poverty, and charity, and became a nun.

Some years later, seeds of dissatisfaction with her cloistered life began to grow, and she became increasingly interested in the reform movement sparked by Luther. When she and other nuns within her orbit read Luther's criticisms of monastic life (thanks to the miracle of the printing press), she questioned the validity of separating oneself from everyday society as an act of supreme religious devotion and virtue. Luther espoused living a Christian life in whatever vocational position one might choose. Since he found no Scriptural basis for monastic vows, he advocated that it is not necessary to live a cloistered religious life to be of optimal service to God and to others. This message reverberated widely, and the halls of the monasteries began to echo even more for lack of occupants.

Six years after the posting of the 95 Theses, Luther helped devise a scheme, at their insistence, for Katharina and eleven other nuns to escape the convent. The conspiracy involved having the nuns hide inside empty pickled-fish barrels stowed on a delivery wagon. They were secretly and *hastily whisked beyond the walls of their religious captivity. It was a courageous and odoriferous escape!*

Like arranging homes for a litter of abandoned felines, Luther was instrumental in finding families, jobs, and/or spouses for the newly liberated nuns. Katharina was in line to potentially marry two different suitors, but marrying a former nun was considered a crime; matchmaking was, therefore, a complicated challenge. Hicronymus Baumgartner was a student at Wittenberg University; Katharina was enamored with him, but his family disallowed him to marry a former nun, believing it would taint him and his family's honor. Then she was courted by Pastor Glatz, but she would not have him. In the end, she insisted she would only have Martin.

Luther hadn't even considered the possibility of marrying Katharina, or anyone else, for any number of reasons, including the fact that he was branded an outlaw and could well be martyred at any moment. This certainly would not be fair to Katharina, or, if they were to be so blessed, for their children. Besides, he was forty-one years old, and she was twenty-six. Such an age difference.

Finally, Martin relented and concluded that marriage "would please his father, rile the pope, cause the angels to laugh, and the devils to weep." Luther's father Hans and mother Margarethe must have been overwhelmed with joy at the prospect of having grandchildren, after having been resigned for many years that their son the monk would never be a father. (Many a grandparent has expressed the sentiment that, even greater than children, grandchildren are a most wonderful blessing. Of course, the latter is quite dependent on the former. One must first partake of the main course before proceeding to the dessert.)

Once the decision was made, Martin and Katharina were officially married within two weeks, only mentioning the plan to very few friends. Perhaps Luther didn't inform very many in his circle right away because he feared they might try to stop him; they probably would have had reservations about Luther getting married, thinking it might hurt the reformation movement, causing a whiff of scandal.

The Luthers immediately took up residence in the Black Cloister—a cavernous former dormitory and educational institution for Augustinian friars studying in Wittenberg. (Once having been there for seven years, it was donated to them by John, Elector of Saxony, brother of Frederick the Wise.) This expansive residence afforded them the ability to take in rent-paying boarders, raise their own vegetables and fruit, breed live-stock, and brew their own beer—all of which Katie administered with efficiency and know-how. With Katie taking upon herself the duties of running the household, Martin was free to write, have meetings, preach, travel, and attend to growing demands related to the reform movement.

The relationship of Martin and Katharina Luther was much more than a romantic union, as any enduring marriage is likely to be.

Katharina was a seminal woman, especially for the archaic time in which she lived. Generally, women in medieval times were not leaders, managers, landlords, or business partners. They were subjugated by their husbands or by other men in their family or community. In the church, they served subordinate roles, e.g. as nuns, housekeepers, or cooks (or concubines). Women were regarded as second-class citizens, not accorded much in the way of human rights, recognition, or respect. The gentler sex had to acquiesce to the power around her in order to survive in a harsh and unjust world.

Katie Luther was the somewhat unacknowledged, lovelier, and sub-tler half of the bold and brash reformer—the ballast in the familial vessel. Her strong and diverse role within the intricate Luther household could be regarded as a small stepping stone toward women achieving greater authority and privilege in society—a mere short stride on an incremental march toward having more equal rights compared to men.

A man of his time, Martin certainly would not have articulated this perspective. The division of labor within his household was a prag-matic development rather than a philosophical one, allowing him to focus on his work.

Contrary to accepted church tenets, he believed that "marriage is essentially a secular affair...subject to secular government, as are clothing and food, house and home." He asserted that there are no instances "in the New Testament in which Christ or the apostles interested themselves in such matters." To him, "marriage is a civic matter. It is really not, together with all its circumstances, the business of the church. It is so only when a matter of conscience is involved."

Additionally, he stated, "A truly good wife is a gift of God…and is not found accidentally and without divine guidance. On the contrary, she is a gift of God and does not come, as the heathen imagine, in answer to our planning and judging.

"Conjugal love excels all other love. The love toward one's spouse burns like a fire and seeks nothing but the person of the spouse. It says: I do not desire what is yours; I desire neither silver nor gold, neither this nor that; I desire you yourself; I want you entirely or not at all. All other love seeks something else than the person of the loved one. Conjugal love alone wants the entire person of the loved one…"

Luther also spoke directly and candidly about sex. He believed that human beings are created for sex life. "The word of God 'Be fruitful and multiply' (Gen. 1:28) is not a mere commandment. It refers to a divine work that we cannot hinder or forgo, a work that is as necessary as the fact that I am a man, and more necessary than eating and drinking, digesting food, and sleeping and waking. It is planted in our nature and kind just as well as are the members required for it. Therefore, just as God commands no one to be man or woman but creates them to be such, so he also does not need to command them to multiply but causes them inevitably to multiply. Moreover, if a person wants to prevent it, it still is not prevented but is carried on anyway by fornication, adultery, and self-defilement; for nature is at work here, not caprice" (W 10 II, 276—E 16, 511—SL 10, 600).

Human sexuality is a topic upon which a multi-volume set of encyclopedias could be devoted, or about which a hundred hours of (controversial) sermons could be presented. Suffice it to say that Luther believed human beings are programmed for sex and that it is normal and natural. He disagreed with the notion that clergy should be celibate, that they should not marry, since this is contradictory to the very nature of being human. Celibacy among clergy had not always been a required discipline. The early church had no definitive rules against marriage for clergy, and for many years, bachelorhood was viewed simply as an ideal observance of an ascetic life, just as (apparently) Jesus and the Apostle Paul did not marry. In the fourth century, the Council of Elvira stipulated that married clergy should abstain from having sex with their wives, and the Second Lateran Council, held in 1139, forbade marriage among clergy and encouraged celibacy. By inference, if marriage was prohibited, then sex was as well, because the church does not condone sex outside of marriage. Undoubtedly, it has been a vague, confusing, and mostly harmful "requirement" which, in truth, has not been an imperative at all. What good is a rule or a so-called discipline if very few observe it? Hypothetically speaking, if the church prohibited sleeping, one would be compelled to steal away to a secret spot for a much-needed nap. If eating and drinking were prohibited, everyone—including priests, cardinals, bishops, and even the pope himself—would be obliged to tiptoe around seeking refreshment, if not in one's own kitchen, surely in the neighbor's. And this would likely happen in the wee hours, under the cloak of darkness and secrecy, to avoid discovery. More manipulation, human frailty, and folly…and religious hypocrisy—a flagrant example of why Luther could not suppress his criticisms of the church and the pope.

*****

Kyle and Carla are very much ready to begin the next chapter in their life together. Although their respective pasts and difficult addiction experiences have become less of a preoccupation, their struggles and victories have readied them to become full-fledged therapists and caregivers. They have chosen a path of sensibility and positivism, knowing full well there is a lurking potential that past behaviors will revisit them. And that would be disastrous without question. Together they will face the world. And stay sober.

On July 4—USA Independence Day—Kyle and Carla, recognizing the irony of simultaneously marking the occasion of their own independence, visit Mom and Dad at their home for a casual barbeque; they take homemade potato salad and chocolate cake (Carla's favorite family recipe) to the gathering.

After the delicious meal of grilled marinated London broil, barbecued chicken, mixed green salad, and potato salad, the foursome relaxes under the blue-striped awning, enjoying the warmth of summer and the soothing sounds of nature. They converse about a wide assortment of topics, including the recent wedding.

Maritza says, "This cake is amazing! It's so moist and perfect. What's the secret?"

"It's coffee," Carla answers. "Who thought to add coffee to a cake recipe? But it works, right?"

David interjects, "Boy, I'll say. It's almost as good as your wedding cake!"

"I know a lot of couples are forgoing the wedding cake in favor of other kinds of desserts," Carla states, "but I've always liked the idea of a cake. It's tradition! People seemed to really enjoy it."

"It was such a special day," Maritza says. "The wedding was so wonderful and perfect—the weather was superb; the ceremony flowed like clockwork."

David interjects, "And only one whistling organ cypher snuck in during the prelude music, and not at all thereafter, thank goodness!" Then he thinks to himself, *I wish the bridesmaids would have worn gowns that didn't show off those grotesque tattoos. Guess I'm old-fashioned. I just don't get the point of that. Kids today!*

Maritza gushes, "The whole thing was a perfect blend of the old and the new, of tradition combined with a creative and personal touch. I especially liked the new song that Kyle and his friend Randy wrote together, and which Randy played on his guitar. 'Love of my life; it may be a cliché! Love of my life...I'll say it anyway.' Not exactly a sacred text, but from the heart, that's for sure. Randy is a really good singer!"

Kyle says, "He sure is. Carla and I met him at our counseling group years ago. Oops, I wasn't supposed to say that! Narcotics *Anonymous!* Oh well, that was so long ago. I'm sure he wouldn't care. At any rate, he's on a really good path right now, it seems, playing in a Christian rock band and traveling around the country with his Christian brothers and sisters. He even has his own recording studio. What an inspiring success story...one which he shares freely as he interacts with his audiences. That's part of what makes their concerts so popular. His life's journey truly resonates with people."

Maritza responds, "That's just amazing, isn't it? The world needs 'ministers' like Randy today—modern-day evangelists who aren't shy about sharing their story. Hopefully, people take his message to heart and avoid trouble. His calling is really a 'music ministry,' isn't it?"

David adds, "In a lot of ways, what Randy is doing is perfect timing; it's a time when the world urgently needs to hear his inspiring story. And the fact that we live in this amazing era of technology whereby his message of redemption can be circulated far and wide, literally touching millions of people—there's Instagram, Facebook, Spotify, YouTube. So many alternatives to get the word out."

Maritza steps up and gives the impression of being rather obtuse. "It reminds me of how the printing press allowed Martin Luther's message to be circulated far and wide."

Everyone else gasps in unison, "*What?*"

"That's sooo random, Mom," Kyle observes.

David says, "There you go again, bringing everything back to Martin Luther! You are obsessed with that guy, I think sometimes! You think today's technology is the equivalent of the printing press. I get it. Other people wouldn't, but I get it."

Kyle says, "Mom, you crack me up."

"Too funny," Carla agrees and abruptly shifts back to talking about Randy's band. "There is one thing that's missing in Randy's approach, and hopefully Kyle and I can do our part to fill that gap. As important and powerful as the larger message is, it's critical that people are affected in a *personal* way, which is what Kyle and I aim to do. Truly, it's in one-on-one or small group situations or in close relationships where healing can really happen. It must be personal. Otherwise, restoration is easily overshadowed by insecurity and doubt. By human frailty."

Kyle adds, "The need is so large for the kind of work we plan to do, there's little chance we'll run out of work—Carla doing drug counseling and me doing family therapy. The only two vocations with higher potential demand might be law enforcement and tattoo removal—enforcing laws, pursuing criminals, and punishing them..."

Carla completes Kyle's thought, "Or undoing a youthful indiscretion...not envisioning that the skull and crossbones tattoo might end up looking like Edvard Munch's painting, *The Scream,* in twenty-five years."

Kyle thinks, "Wow, I really love that girl!"

David asks, "How is it you know about *The Scream?*"

Carla thinks about it and answers, "Well, *The Simpsons,* of course! Homer and Marge! D'oh! Ha ha! Actually, I had to take art appreciation as an elective in college, and we learned all about this iconic modern-day equivalent of Leonardo da Vinci's *Mona Lisa.* When I look at this painting, I see the anxiety and pain many troubled souls have in the world today. It's so powerful and expressive. I just love it!"

"Did you know," David asks, "that it recently sold at art auction for something like $120 million?"

"That's just nuts!" Kyle says.

Maritza gives her input. "That would pay for an awful lot of therapy sessions, wouldn't it?"

Kyle says, "True that!"

After a couple moments, pausing to carefully choose her words, Maritza takes the pulpit. "You know, I just want to say that David and I are so proud of you both. You've turned yourselves around, climbed some very steep mountains. As Dad would say, you've crossed the Rubicon! You've transitioned from a state of self-centeredness to being outwardly focused. Caring for people, listening to them, and helping them takes grit and unwavering commitment. And resilience and genuine compassion. At times, it can be a source of frustration or it can be so satisfying, changing people's lives. It's a mindset that can't be taught; either you're programmed that way or you're not. The fact that you are is a gift and a blessing…for yourselves, for others, and for us as parents. You are or will be helpers and healers. I can't wait to see what the future holds!"

David agrees. "I could not have said it better myself, especially that 'Rubicon' part. Definitely sounds like something I'd say."

Kyle asks, "What does that even mean anyway?"

Maritza answers, "Oh, it's just an old saying."

"Is it something Luther said?" Carla asks.

Maritza laughs. "Believe it or not, no, I don't think so. Anyway, I just had to say that we're so proud and happy. God has blessed us, and I am eternally grateful."

Kyle says, "Thanks, Mom! We're proud of you, too!" He and Carla give her a big hug. David joins the family embrace.

Maritza glances over their shoulders and sees someone walking by the fence near the corner of their property. While the others clean up and take the leftover food and table settings back into air-conditioned comfort, Maritza walks quickly over to the fence to investigate who is loitering nearby. She thinks she recognizes the person but wants to make sure.

CHAPTER 26

Hanging Around

Her nagging suspicion is confirmed. It's that rat, Marty. She hurries out to the sidewalk to confront him.

Like a mama bear prepared to defend her young cubs, she challenges him straight on. "What are you doing here, hanging around this neighborhood? Get out of here right now!"

Marty answers, "Hey, I'm just out for a stroll, and I happened to wander into this lovely neighborhood. I had no idea you lived here… Kyle's meddling mom. Seems to me you and Kyle have a similar inability to mind your own business. It's a free country; I can walk around here if I want."

"Look, Marty," Maritza tries to reason, "I want nothing more than for you to get your life on track. You must have had a difficult life. I have no idea about everything you've experienced. The fact that you have shown up at my house, looking like you're stalking my family, tells me that you are looking for trouble. Apparently, you haven't learned a damn thing about obeying the law or about personal responsibility or I don't know what else. You need to get out of here…*right now!*"

Marty grimaces. "Wow. Yeah, you're absolutely right about that…you have no idea what I've been through."

Exasperated, Maritza says, "You sound like a friggin five year old. Wah, wah, wah! When are you going to grow up and stop making excuses for your life? What is it going to take for you to stop feeling sorry for yourself and get on with it?"

"Boy, aren't you the compassionate preacher?" Marty asks. "Do you treat every lost lamb you come across this way?"

Maritza's blood approaches a boiling point. "You're not a lost lamb. You're a grown man with maturity issues. Have you ever thought about turning to God, admitting you are powerless against whatever it is that is troubling you deep in your heart?"

Marty responds, "Religion never did much for me. I don't get it...I wasn't raised that way. Seems like a bunch of bullshit, really. Besides, I've done so much stuff, I've hurt so many people—some for good reasons, some just for sport—I just don't see how I can change at this point. What's the big deal anyway? My life sucks, plain and simple."

"Marty," Maritza sighs and says calmly, "if *you* don't see the point of changing, no one can do it for you. All I can say is, I've seen miracles of faith happen. I've witnessed unexpected redemption in places where hopelessness, hate, and genuine evil have previously resided. God's redeeming love is a gift for anyone, even for the lost wretches of the world."

"Even for a wretch like me?" Marty asks sarcastically. "Isn't that from a song or something?"

Finally, Maritza states, "Look, I don't have anything else to say to you now other than you have to move on, get out of here. If you don't, I will have no choice but to call the cops."

"Okay, okay, I'll move on. You don't have to be such a bee-atch about it. Geez."

Firmly and calmly, Maritza orders, "Move it!"

Maritza returns to her family inside the house. Marty walks on. He thinks while glancing back toward Maritza and her family, *What is it about these Christians that they keep on trying to change me?*

CHAPTER 27

•◦◦•─────◦─────•◦◦•

Fireworks and Lightning and Thunder

There is some doubt about whether the Fourth of July fireworks will even take place. It's been a typically hot July with high humidity and a looming threat of thunderstorms. Everyone is hopeful the fireworks can be pulled off. It's just never the same if the fireworks happen at a later date other than July 4.

At 9:15 p.m., Kyle suggests they all move outside since the fireworks are about to commence. In previous years, they've viewed the fireworks from the backyard since the home sits on a bluff. It's a showcase definitely worth the price of admission!

As they stroll outside together with lawn chairs and mosquito repellant in hand, David asks Maritza, "Who was that you were talking with earlier?"

She answers, "Oh, no one really. Only that lug-head Marty."

"Marty!" David exclaims. "What was that devil doing loitering around our neighborhood? As if I didn't know."

"Let's not dwell on that right now," Maritza says. "Let's enjoy the rest of our family time together and the show that's about to begin."

David looks up and sees stars clearly in the east, but clouds obscure the celestial heavens to the west. "Looks like the sky's pretty clear where the fireworks will be set off. Hopefully, the clouds won't roll in too quickly, ruining the show." He sees flashes of light to the west. "Uh-oh. That's not looking too promising."

Momentarily, the first comet of fire speeds to its lofty destination, like a missile launched from Cape Canaveral. It explodes with a bang so loud they can feel it on their chests. The display continues with fifteen minutes of glorious sparkles and explosions of different hues and patterns and at different heights to the delight of the closely-knit audience. There is a brief pause before the grand finale which suddenly spills upward in a cornucopia of spectacular multicolored lights and rapid fire explosions.

All of a sudden, there is a brilliant flash of light accompanied by a frightening canon-like bang twice as loud as the loudest of the fireworks. Obviously, this was a lightning strike, and it hit very close by.

Kyle exclaims, "Holy crap! That was really close!"

Carla says, "Nature's fireworks! No one can compete with that!"

After a moment, David stands up to look closer in the direction of the lightning strike.

"I see smoke." He points. "Looks like it's coming from the apartments over there."

Maritza is unnerved. "That's where my friend, Rachel the cantor, lives. Oh, dear God, I hope everyone's all right." She asks David, "Do you think we should go there, make sure everyone's okay?"

Emergency sirens ramp up in the distance.

David answers, "Let's let the professionals do their job. We'd just get in the way."

CHAPTER 28

•◦●▬▬▬▬◦▬▬▬▬●◦•

Smoke and Fire

At about the same time…

Still wandering about and stewing on his irritating encounter with Maritza, Marty thinks to himself as he takes a deep drag on a joint, *Maybe I should rethink getting even with Kyle and Carla. If I hurt them and get caught, I might as well plan to spend the rest of my days in prison. That would not be good, obviously.* He thinks on the possibilities. *Of course, I could make sure there are no witnesses…*

Suddenly, a deafening bang and a blinding light distract Marty from his maniacal thoughts. He is pushed off balance by the incredible force of a lightning strike within a half block of where he's walking. He felt like the sound of it nearly blew out his eardrums.

"Holy f——ing shit! That was close!" He moves closer, quickening his pace. He hears screaming.

As he arrives at the front door of the three-story apartment complex, people are streaming out of the entrance door in a panic. The screaming gets more intense.

Is someone trapped in the building? Marty wonders.

Curiously, he thinks he hears a faint voice. "Go ahead…save them."

"Who said that?" Marty demands. He looks around and sees no one. He is fearful on many levels.

"Go ahead…save them."

"Must have been some bad weed; what the hell?"

"Go ahead…save your sister."

Stunned, Marty exclaims, "Save my sister?"

A stout older gentleman, dressed in antediluvian attire, emerges from amidst the confusion, firmly grabs Marty by the arm and says, "We should go in."

The stranger is so cool and steady in his demeanor, Marty doesn't even think to contradict him. He responds, "Yeah, let's go."

They hurry into the building, negotiating past the people coming out; they climb the stairs to the third floor.

Following the terrifying screams, they locate the source through the thickening smoke, but the apartment door is locked. Marty lunges at the door with all his strength, and it gives way. Smoke billows from the room.

Blinded by the thick choking smoke, Marty and the stranger miraculously locate the helpless victims—an older woman and a young girl, and both have been overcome by the toxic fumes.

The stranger says, "I'll carry this one; you carry the little girl."

Marty embraces the child and carries her out to the hallway and down the stairs. The woman is transported right behind them by Marty's rescuing accomplice, who uses a textbook fireman's carry.

Once outside, the coughing victims are handed off to other *Good Samaritans* from the neighborhood who have arrived to offer assistance.

Then Marty says to the stranger, "I'm going back in. There might be more people trapped inside. I gotta check."

The stranger smiles and nods affirmingly. Marty puts his face in the crook of his arm and pushes forward, back into the smoldering building.

After a few more harrowing seconds, two fire trucks and an ambulance arrive at the chaotic scene. The firemen get to work securing the area, making sure all the residents are safely out of the building. They extend the fire hoses and douse the structure. EMTs attend to the injured.

There is no sign of Marty.

After several more minutes, three firemen emerge from the charred building carrying a limp, motionless body. It is Marty.

Sitting on the edge of a gurney and pulling off her oxygen mask, the older woman, Rachel, points toward the trio of firemen carrying

Marty and excitedly says, "That's the man who rescued my grand-daughter and me! He carried us both at the same time. I have no idea how he did that, but he's a hero! He is our hero!"

An EMT puts the mask back on her and encourages her to calm down. She takes the mask off again and inquires, "Is he going to be all right? Dear God, please let him be okay."

Barely conscious, Marty asks the EMT in a whispering, raspy voice, his strength fading, "Where's the guy that helped me carry those people out? He was just right here. He was dressed kind of weird."

Looking around, the EMT says, "He's delirious. I have no idea what he's talking about."

The professional rescuers frantically attend to Marty, but their herculean efforts are performed in vain. The poisonous hot fumes from burning plastic and paint had filled his lungs in mere minutes, resulting in chronic respiratory distress and heart failure.

Marty is dead.

A shroud is laid over the lifeless body to obscure it from onlookers.

Rachel and her eight-year-old granddaughter, Tabitha, are placed in the ambulance and rushed to the nearby hospital. Their condition is serious, but the EMTs assure them that they will be fine.

The weather becomes increasingly precarious. A furious gyrating wind swoops in, accompanied by drenching rain. The temperature drops ten degrees, and the conspicuous smell of ozone fills the air.

CHAPTER 29

Nature's Fireworks Equal Tragedy

The intense thunderstorm caused the power to blink a couple of times, but thankfully it wasn't knocked out entirely. Queuing up the eleven o'clock local evening news, Maritza and David watch intently, hoping to learn details about the apparent apartment fire across town.

"This is Jenny Singleton reporting live from the scene of a tragic fire at the Parkview Apartments on the city's west side." The articulate and attractive reporter lays out the details of the ill-fated incident. "According to witnesses, a lightning strike hit the building just before 10:00 p.m., igniting the fire. I'm told there are a couple victims who have been taken to St. Luke's Hospital nearby. Their condition is unknown at this point. I've also been informed that, apart from our everyday heroes in the fire and police departments, an individual rescued some of the residents singlehandedly before the first responders arrived. At this point, it appears, tragically, that this individual was overcome with smoke while in the act of saving others. He is the only fatality as far as we know. We cannot confirm his identity until his relatives have been notified." She pauses, as her emotions rise up. "A completely unselfish act on his part. What an incredible individual this must have been! Such unselfish heroism!"

CHAPTER 30

Strange Hero

At midnight, after having received treatment for smoke inhalation and having notified her family about the terrible incident, Rachel sends a text message to her good friend, Maritza, asking her to call her. It's late, but Maritza is still awake. She calls Rachel who explains over the phone what has happened and asks if she would be so kind to pay her a visit the next day.

Maritza says, "I'll clear my calendar. Of course, I'll be there. How's ten o'clock?"

Coughing a little, Rachel responds, "Sounds perfect."

The next morning, Maritza arrives at the hospital to visit Rachel. On her way to Rachel's room, she stops at the nurse's station where she is well-known because of her untold number of pastoral visits. She asks Naomi, the charge nurse, who also happens to be a devout Lutheran and the wife of the county coroner, if she knows who the fire fatality was last night.

"I can't really say," Naomi insists. "You know, HIPAA privacy rules and all that."

Maritza concedes, "I know. I understand. I have a sneaking suspicion I know who it was. Can you at least give me a hint? His first name? If it is who I think it is, he doesn't have any family really."

Naomi gestures to Maritza to come closer. She whispers, "His first name was Martin. I think he went by 'Marty.'"

Based on her phone conversation with Rachel and the description of her improbable rescuer, Maritza is not surprised. Her suspicion is confirmed.

"Thank you, sister," Maritza declares. "You know I'll keep this confidential."

Naomi says, "Keep what?" She smiles like the Cheshire Cat.

Maritza proceeds to Rachel's room; the door is ajar. She knocks while pushing the door open. "May I come in?" She observes that Rachel has an oxygen tube placed under her nostrils.

Rachel answers, "By all means. It's so good to see you. What a nightmare, right?"

"Oh, I'll say! My family and I were watching the fireworks from our house—you know where we live, about a half mile from your place—and we heard the incredible explosive sound of the lightning strike. Then I saw the smoke emanating from your apartment building, and I was so worried about you."

Rachel says, "My granddaughter, Tabitha, and I were watching the fireworks, too, from my little balcony when *POW*, nature's fury hit."

Maritza says, "The power of nature is so incredible, isn't it? Tell me again how you got out."

"Well, I must have been in shock; I was stunned and couldn't think what to do. I just could not move. We were on the balcony, so we had to go back through the apartment to get out. I opened the slider door and saw the smoke. I froze. Tabitha was screaming and frantic, but she's so small, just a child."

Maritza asks, "Is Tabitha okay?"

"Yes, the nurses told me she's doing fine. Although if we had stayed in the building much longer, things would have turned out much worse, no doubt.

"Thankfully, in probably less than a minute, this burly guy bursts into the apartment, throws me over his shoulder and grabs Tabitha. I don't remember much from that point until I was outside. I remember seeing firemen carrying what looked like the same guy out of the building. I was so concerned for him. I hope he's all right. You don't know who he is or what his condition is, do you?"

Maritza pauses and takes a deep breath. "Actually, I do." Tears well up in her eyes. "It's so sad and yet pretty miraculous. He was the only casualty from the fire; he succumbed from the thick toxic smoke."

Rachel sighs, "Oh no. Unbelievable. That is *so terrible!*"

"What's even more incredible," Maritza shares, "is that I know him."

"Oh really, you do?" Rachel responds.

"Yes, he was a very troubled young man. His name was Marty. It's a long story, but he and my son got tangled together years ago, when Kyle was getting into trouble with drugs. Marty was released from prison recently, and I even saw him late in the day yesterday, if you can believe it. We had a brief conversation. I know he was struggling with his past and having difficulty mainstreaming back into the world outside of prison. He was a lost soul and really, really bad news, to be perfectly honest. My impression yesterday was that even in prison, he really hadn't changed or learned much about reclaiming his God-given life. He couldn't fathom turning his life around because he had done so much bad stuff; he had great difficulty coming to terms with that. Hard to appreciate his state of mind, but he was so overloaded with regret and guilt that he felt he was powerless to change. That's my sense of it anyway.

"But there must have been a morsel of goodness in his heart. For him to rescue you and Tabitha so bravely without regard for his own well-being shows there was a caring person inside that caustic exterior. His moral compass was mostly broken, but a small part of it still functioned."

Rachel has been listening intently. She reflectively asks, "So what does Christian theology teach about redemption and the power of God to judge and to condemn? Especially for someone like this young man, Marty. What are his prospects in the afterlife, if there is such a thing?"

Maritza jokes, "I have no earthly idea!" They laugh softly at the irony. "Actually, I do," she continues. "You know, Jesus taught a lot by using stories—parables—and one of the most powerful ones is the story of the 'Prodigal Son.' Are you familiar with it?"

"Yes, I think so," Rachel answers. "It's the story about a son who takes his family inheritance and squanders it on wine, women, and song. Then once he is destitute, he returns to his father to see if he can work as a servant in his house, so he'll at least have food and shelter."

Maritza explains, "And the father greets him joyfully, has a welcoming party, a celebration! This causes some family jealousy and raises a number of interesting questions; but the father focuses mainly on the fact that his son was woefully lost but now, thankfully, is found. It's a powerful message that sums up what God's redeeming love is all about, for us Christians anyway. And the analogy of an earthly father and son makes it that much easier to grasp. What kind of father could turn away a destitute son?"

Rachel says, "It seems similar to the idea of 'atonement,' which involves admitting one's mistakes, expressing regret, repenting, and making amends. Is that part of this story?"

"Well, yes and no," Maritza explains. "I think regret and repenting are an important part of the parable, but the father doesn't say his son has broken all the rules and is now sorry for his mistakes. He doesn't say the son is going to pay back all the money he wasted. He only says that his son was lost and now is found."

Rachel reacts, "Hmm, that really makes my brain hurt. It goes against the grain of what we've been taught since we were children. Sort of like that *quid pro quo* thing we talked about before."

"I agree," Maritza says. "I really want to be positive and believe that God is merciful, even for a wretch like Marty. God's grace and love are truly unconditional."

Rachel scrunches her nose, causing the oxygen tube to dislodge. "I'm gonna have to think on that some more. My eyes are starting to twitch!"

Maritza smiles. "Some food for thought, I suppose." She pauses to think.

Not wanting to overstay her welcome, Maritza says, "Well, I'd better go. Shall I visit you tomorrow?"

"Sure, although I might be discharged tomorrow. I'll let you know."

"And do you have a place to stay? I'm sure you can't return to your apartment."

Rachel answers, "Yes, I can stay with my daughter and son-in-law—Tabitha's parents. It's already been arranged."

Maritza wishes Rachel a speedy recovery, says goodbye, and heads for home.

CHAPTER 31

Sola Gratia

"Hey, David! I'm home!" Maritza announces. In a lilting voice she says, "I've got something amazing to tell you!"

After settling in, she updates David on Rachel's condition and tells him all about Marty and the miraculous rescue.

David processes the details and responds, "That's a story which is almost beyond belief. Not to sound glib, but that guy, Marty, really went out with a bang! Almost seems like a parable to me."

Maritza says, "You know, you're right. A modern-day parable! Guess we could conclude yet again that the good Lord works in mysterious ways."

"Mysterious ways indeed!" David agrees. "Maybe it's an example of how God and his host of angels work behind the scenes, even when we're rebellious and disobedient, to bring his lost sheep back into the fold." He pauses a moment, then says, "Let's talk some more later. Right now, I need to get to class to impart my cosmic historical knowledge to a multitude of starry-eyed, aspiring, bright young scholars. By the way, Kyle left a note for you on the desk in your study."

"Okay, thanks," Maritza responds. "I'll check it out." She pours herself a glass of iced tea. Then she walks into her study and picks up the folded note with an accompanying printed page.

She reads:

Dear Mom,

I was inspired to write this poem about grace. I included some Latin to make it sound 'churchy.' I think you'll like it…hope so, anyway.

Love,
Kyle

Sola Gratia:
Sola Gratia, Sola Gratia
By grace alone, not by our well-intentioned deeds
*   or bequests*
Not by caring or hoping or prayerful requests
Only a gift, given you because a loving Creator
Gave you life, what could be greater?
Could a loving mother contradict her nature?
Would a father rather love
A total stranger?

Sola Gratia, Sola Gratia
By grace alone, not helping others or by feeding the poor
Not by begging or beseeching face down on the floor
God is a painter, builder, sculptor, and a gifted
*   composer*
He is not to be won over
Doing good is not the measure
Set your mind at ease, avoid the noise and pressure
God is Love; God is Love—
Unearned, unmeasured.

Choked up with emotion, Maritza whispers to herself, *That's great, son. Really, really great. Unbelievably great!* She walks across the room and drops into her overstuffed chair to read the poem several times to savor its meaning, to fully grasp its remarkable and liberating message. Then as she sets the paper down, she notices there is more writing on the back:

> Mom, I wrote this snippet specifically with
> you in mind…something for you to meditate on.
> Peace out! —K.

> *Throw your worry in the water*
> *Float your burdens out to the sea*

Meanwhile…

Beyond the infinite and inscrutable expanse of the magnificent star-filled universe, a loud, over-the-top welcoming home party with bright lights, beautiful music, dancing, and singing is taking place. A lost lamb has found his way home. It is as though he never left.

The end.

QUESTIONS FOR GROUP STUDY/DISCUSSION

Can you identify at least six redemption stories in the book? (There are more.) Discuss the path each character traveled and how their redemption is assessed.

How can we love and forgive someone if they have done something terribly wrong to us? What might forgiveness look like?

Is there redemption for someone who has done numerous bad things in life and one *really good* thing? Conversely, is there redemption for someone who has done numerous good things but one *really bad* one?

If a person is compelled to do evil things due to influences beyond one's control (i.e., addiction, poverty, poisonous relationships, dysfunctional family life, life-shattering tragedy, depression, etc.), how do you think God assesses the value of such a life? Can God's love and grace transcend the evil which can consume a person, especially when the individual may be powerless against it?

Do you believe God has the capability to influence lives and events? If yes, what does this look like?

Do you think history is important? Why or why not? What about tradition?

Why is the law important (both civil and religious)? Where does the idea of punishment for having broken the law originate? Is it effective? What purpose does it serve? What do secular law and religious law have in common?

If people of different beliefs (religious or other) dig in their heels, judge others in an antagonistic, adversarial, and sanctimonious way, where does it lead? What are the possible outcomes?

Why do you think people fall prey to drug and alcohol abuse? What are some key factors which could prevent addictive behaviors? What tactics can lead an addicted person to recovery and restoration?

Why are many mainline churches struggling to survive? Is the church relevant today? Why or why not?

How do religious and secular groups in your community collaborate to serve the poor, the needy, the addicted, the imprisoned, the lost? How can these efforts be improved?

ACKNOWLEDGEMENTS

With sincere and heartfelt gratitude, I would like to acknowledge those who provided inspiration and graciously contributed in ways big and small to the creation of this book with feedback, wise counsel, and professional expertise—Tim Averill, Sharon Barshinger, Michael Bennethum, Maritza Torres Dolich, Ese Duke, Rob Ernst, John Flamish, Robin Flores, Rick Grube, James Christopher Heist, David John "DJ" Kormanik, Gina Kormanik, Donna Jacobson, Robert Lawson, Martin Luther, William Maxon, Kerrie McCarthy Armbruster, Ann Shade, Rabbi Seth Phillips, Walter Wagner, Christ Lutheran Church Chancel Choir, Marc DeBoeser, Kara DeBoeser, and most especially my beloved wife, Catherine.

KDB

RESOURCES

Anyone seeking professional help with recovery from drug or alcohol addiction may consult these resources:

www.restinjesus.org
www.celebraterecovery.com
www.samhsa.gov
www.drugfree.org
www.aa.org
www.na.org
www.al-anon.org
www.nar-anon.org
www.williamwhitepapers.com/pr/dlm_uploads/Multiple-Pathways-of-Recovery-Guide-2018.pdf

ABOUT THE AUTHOR

Photo credit: Grace Heavner

Having faced disappointment and heartbreak in life, like nearly everyone, the author has developed a broad philosophical perspective over many years as a person of faith, laboring as a professional church musician, teacher, parent, and as a witness of God's grace. His faith in himself and in God has been severely tested. He has witnessed, among family and friends, the horrors of drug and alcohol addiction. He has observed a disconcerting exodus of people from mainline churches. In an age when truth seems elusive, when meaning is difficult to assess, when complex questions continue to perplex our society, the author was compelled to write this modern-day parable to advance deeper understanding and human empathy. The author relates an intricately interwoven story—highlighting themes of faith, redemption, God's love and grace, addiction/recovery, loss, hope... and history.

CPSIA information can be obtained
at www.ICGtesting.com
Printed in the USA
BVHW041636300322
632853BV00016B/1224